SKIING
IS ONLY A GAME

the six-day programme
that will revolutionise your skiing

SKIING
IS ONLY A GAME

Peter Lightfoot

cartoons by Mike Peyton

Fernhurst Books

First published 1985
Revised edition 1987
Fernhurst Books, 31 Church Road, Hove, East Sussex

ISBN 0 906754 20 8

Composition by A & G Phototypesetters, Knaphill
Printed and bound in Great Britain by Hollen Street
Press, Slough

ACKNOWLEDGEMENTS

There are many people without whose help this book would never have been written. Special thanks are due to:

Edwina, my wife, for her hours of patient listening and advice;

Ali Ross of the British Association of Ski Instructors for the many original ideas he has shared with me over the years, and which are also expounded in his book *How we Learned to Ski*;

Claudia Viviani of the Canadian Ski Instructors Association, Martin Lemprière of the New Zealand Ski Instructors Alliance and Sir John Whitmore, who have read the manuscript and made valuable contributions;

Richard Jarvis of Sportline Ltd, UK importers of Head Skis, and Oliver Hart of Salomon UK Ltd for their generous support of our courses;

Branko Perkov, Marketing Director of Val Thorens, France, for his hospitality;

Roger Seydoux of the Villars Tourist Office and Gustav Chable of the Swiss Ski School, Villars for their support and cooperation;

the Ski Club of Great Britain for their constant assistance and help;

Reg and Betty Collett and Doris and Brian Beirne for providing me with a quiet retreat in which to write;

and all those pupils with whom I've had the pleasure of skiing over the years and from whom I've learned so much.

Photo credits

The publishers gratefully acknowledge permission to reproduce the following photographs:

Berghaus – pages 32, 34.

Villars Tourist Office – page 8.

Dynastar Look Nordica – page 17.

Mark Junak – pages 6, 21, 22, 27, 45, 81, 89, 93.

Sport International – pages 58/9, 64, 75, 76.

The cover photograph is by Mark Shapiro, courtesy of Berghaus Ltd, and the cover design is by Behram Kapadia.

Contents

Preface

Learning is always accumulative. Since I began skiing twenty-five years ago very many people, including ski teachers from many countries, have contributed to my understanding of the most effective and enjoyable ways to assist others to become the sort of skier they want to be. It was however the 'Inner Game' that had the greatest import and influence upon the way I teach – and learn.

In 1974 American tennis coach Timothy Gallwey wrote *The Inner Game of Tennis* which was destined to become the best-selling tennis book ever. Three years later he co-authored with Bob Kriegel a book called *Inner Skiing*, and offered courses in Inner Skiing to American skiers and instructors. Inner skiing courses were then organized, developed and expanded in Europe over a number of years by Sarah Ferguson, 1978 British Freestyle Champion, and ex-racing driver Sir John Whitmore. In 1983 my company, Ski Skills Ltd of which Sir John is a director, acquired the European rights for Inner Skiing and continues to run courses throughout each winter in the Alps.

Inner Skiing has caused me to alter radically my thinking about teaching and learning skiing and to recognise the human factors which govern the learning process and which will always have a high priority over matters of technique, style and 'doing it right'. The 'proper technique' can and does develop naturally and painlessly given the opportunity and the right environment.

This book is an expression of this principle – one that challenges the belief that anything worth while, including success on the ski slopes, can only be achieved by effort and self-sacrifice.

Above all it is a product of my experience and that of our team of coaches as we have worked closely with hundreds of skiers of all standards from beginners to experts during the past three seasons.

This book is designed to be of practical value to you, to present an approach to skiing which will be of immense benefit to you the next time you go to the mountains, and to ensure that these benefits will stay with you for the rest of your life.

I wish you happy and successful skiing.

Peter Lightfoot

Opposite: the Swiss resort of Villars, home of the Ski Skills Courses.

Introduction

There is a lot to learning to ski! How you approach it can determine both how you succeed and how much you enjoy it. Learning is not the same as 'being taught'. This book is not going to 'teach' you to ski! It can however be the most powerful *learning* tool you've ever experienced.

LEARNING

Remember how you first learned to ski? Here's how I first learned to ski 25 years ago:

My ski teacher was a very strict but amiable Swiss who knew how to ski very well and who wanted us to ski well too. He would give us verbal instructions of how to perform a certain manoeuvre on skis, something like: "Traverse with the uphill shoulder, hip and ski slightly advanced. Keep an upright position while angling the uphill ski with the downhill ski weighted then, with a quick downhill movement, place the downhill stick with the inner shoulder, hip and ski advanced. Transfer the weight completely to the outer ski by a strong pull of the inner ski and draw the de-weighted inner ski smoothly parallel to the outer ski, counter-rotate outwards and transfer the weight on to the outer ski"!

He would follow that instruction with a demonstration of what he meant, producing an immaculate turn whilst the class all tried to see what he had done and to recognise the instructions he had previously given. Then he would invite each of us in turn to copy the movement he had just made, while we all watched waiting for our 'go'. As each skier descended there was a feeling of being 'on test' in front of your teacher and your friends. You were determined to do well and not let yourself down. When we reached the instructor we would be given a critique of our performance. This usually highlighted the things we had done 'wrong', so we would concentrate on these aspects the next time.

After another couple of 'goes' I would start to compare my turns with those of the teacher. I thought his was the only way to turn and I was pleased when I did a turn which seemed 'right' and I was frustrated and disappointed when I did one that seemed 'wrong'.

The teacher in an effort to correct an obvious fault would criticize something I was doing. Not welcoming criticism, I would try harder not to do it again. If I did I would criticize myself and even tell myself to do better next time. Sometimes I could be heard shouting out to myself "Don't be so STUPID", as again I would do the very thing I was trying not to do.

Because I loved to ski I didn't mind the way I was learning, and I didn't mind getting depressed occasionally and wondering if I would ever ski well. To me that was what learning was all about, and I wanted badly to learn to ski.

Do you recognise this pattern? Is it similar to your experiences in learning to ski – frustration and hard work with some glorious bits in between, but you got there in the end?

This is how I learnt to ski! Did it work? The answer has to be yes. I could certainly ski, and before I could not.

So if it worked, why am I writing a book which advocates a different approach? Well, the horse and cart worked and so did the town-crier. The elements which made them work have since been developed to fulfil much more of their potential. By leaving out what was thought *then* to be necessary we have retained the essence of their purpose but improved considerably on their efficiency, giving us the motor car and the radio. And we're not finished yet! The purpose of this book, and the 'Ski Skills' courses on which it is based, is to select the elements which actually produce our learning and develop them to the maximum, and leave out those elements which are often thought to be necessary, but – as we shall see – can and do get in the way.

"BEND ZEE KNEES"

What skier has not heard that shouted at them countless times! What does it *really* mean? Is it helpful advice? OR is it going to hinder our progress as a skier? Let's examine this immortal phrase and we can decide the value for ourselves.

Imagine you are skiing under the eye of your instructor. You have all the anxieties of unfamiliarity with a risky activity, and you are anxious to perform as accurately as you can the movements demonstrated by your instructor. This double anxiety produces, quite naturally, some tension in the body. Your legs are stiff and your ankle joints have little movement. Your weight is inclined to be too far back where you may feel you are more able to control your speed. The instructor sees what's happening and particularly that you are not:

- allowing your body to absorb the contours of the hill;
- letting your ankle flex to help produce an effective edge;
- aware that your weight is so far back that most of the skis' edges are off the snow.

In fact a detailed analysis would provide ten other vital comments that didn't look 'right' too!

So now you are not merely a skier, you are a skier with several problems! The teacher highlights one symptom and shouts out *"Bend Zee Knees"!* Why? Because he knows that when *he* skis his knees are supple and flexible, and automatically absorb the various pressures put upon them. His experience of what works for *him* suddenly becomes *a rule to be obeyed.*

You may greet this advice in two ways. You either say to yourself "But I *am* bending my knees" and genuinely feel it is superfluous advice, or you start bending your knees up and down merely to carry out the instruction, regardless of outside factors. You end up even more tense, even less confident, bobbing up and down like a deranged rabbit. As soon as one thing is 'right' something else seems to go 'wrong'. Frustration soon sets in!

AT LAST HE'S BENDING THEM

How much learning was there in this example?

Clearly not very much, but there was *potential for learning.* It just wasn't being expressed. Let's look at how the potential for learning was wasted;

- There could have been feedback from your instructor about the tension in your legs.
- You yourself could have noticed the tension in your legs. How much? Where? When? Any difference between left and right turns?
- You could have experimented and observed with a natural curiosity what happens when you do bend your knees. Without forcing them to perform to some preconceived notion, there is *potential* for learning in just doing and seeing what happens!
- In merely being completely absorbed by what the knees are doing the rest of the body could be just allowed to get on with the skiing.
- There is learning potential in discovering that although the stiffness of your knees has been criticised, what is really absorbing *your* interest is the

fact that you feel this slope is too steep for you and you would prefer to find another route.

- By observing your instructor skiing in front, you could simply absorb the image of flexibility and rhythm which you see, and then let your body ski in that image.

Do you see what I mean by the potential for learning? That one instruction had it all, but it was simply hidden, successfully camouflaged!

There is nothing wrong with the instruction to 'BEND ZE KNEES'. All the learning you want and need is there. But does it work? The approach we adopt on our courses, the 'Ski Skills approach' if you like, is to highlight, expand, develop and use to the full the *real* learning potentials that lie behind such a basic instruction. The Ski Skills coaches aim to guide the pupils to concentrate *entirely* on the real learning whilst at the same time helping them to recognise and deal with the interferences and obstructions that get in the way.

Incredible changes can and do take place every day when the learning is as undiluted, and as individual as this. You will discover this for yourself as you read and try out some of the games, drills and examples in this book.

What interferes with our learning?

What *does* get in the way of our learning? Let's be clear what we mean by learning, as this will help us be clear on what gets in the way. You can think of learning in two ways:

1 When we are born we know nothing, and like an empty jug we spend our life being filled up with facts and information. As products of our environment we are moulded by the experiences of life, as clay is moulded by the potter.

OR

2 We arrive on this planet with as much potential within us to be a skier, or for that matter to be a successful and fulfilled human being, as does an acorn have the potential to become an oak tree.

An acorn won't become an oak tree on its own. It will need water, light, warmth and nourishment, and eventually the oak tree will emerge. Do you say about a small sapling "that's a lousy oak tree" or do you recognise that here is a fine oak tree at an early stage of its development? Similarly, we will not become an accomplished skier on our own. We need guidance,

encouragement and clarity of purpose to enable the potential skier within us to emerge.

However, the potential to be the skier you want to be is ALREADY within you. It just needs to be allowed to develop!

If you subscribe to theory (1) your skiing future will depend upon the information, advice, tips, criticisms and 'help' given you by others.

If you subscribe to (2) you will recognise that you already have what you need in order to perform or learn and that these additional contributions are of secondary importance, indeed they can and often do get in the way!

How do these interferences get in the way?

When you are out skiing, have any of the following thoughts entered your head?

- "I think I'm the best skier in this group, I wonder if they think so too?"
- "I must put more weight on the outside ski and keep my knee flexible".
- "Jim is doing better than me today – he hasn't been skiing as long as I have and now I can't keep up with him."
- "This slope is a bit too steep!"
- "I'm going to show my instructor what I can do."
- "I'll just do six turns under the chair lift."
- "I'm determined to get it right this time, now what did he say I've got to do?"
- "So I've just done 40 linked turns in the powder, but as usual I lost my rhythm in the middle."

Perhaps you've had similar thoughts. It seems that whenever we ski something inside us, some little voice, is giving us a running commentary. Have you heard it? This little voice tells us "bend your left leg", so we try to bend our left leg. It tells us "your friend is watching you from the chair lift" so we stiffen up in apprehension and try and put on a good performance. It tells us "try harder" so we grip our poles tighter! It tells us "don't be so scared" so our mouth goes even drier. It tells us "you're a hopeless skier" so we perform hopelessly. It tells us "you're a fantastic skier" and you crash into the lift line. You've heard it too?

I call this 'the little voice' but it's really our ego having its say. Our ego is the part of our brain that likes to think it's in control of us and the situation we're in. When you start to listen to it and respond to its suggestions it can actually start to *take* control whether you like it or not!

Skiing is a natural activity performed in an arena of natural elements, snow, gravity, pulls of forces. Our bodies can learn to respond to this natural, but new, environment if trusted to learn how for itself. Our egos, ever confident and knowing, would have us believe that *they* hold the answers to acquiring the technique and persist in offering us their advice!

Try this experiment

If you ever travel by the London Underground, or on a bus, here's an easy experiment to try. Find a space so there's some room around you, but also where there is a safety rail within easy grabbing distance. When the train or bus is moving leave go of the rail and just balance, keeping your feet still. Not too difficult, is it? It takes perhaps half a minute to get used to the strangeness of the sensation. Your body is inclined well forward if you are facing the direction of travel, isn't it? Notice the pressures in your feet and the many small muscle movements you are making. Notice your hands. Are they

against your sides or away from your body? Notice your knees, are they locked straight or flexed and absorbing the motion?

Do you see how quickly your body learns to adapt to a new environment? You might question how natural it is to stand on a tube train without holding on, but yet the response of the body was entirely natural. It didn't need instructions or advice on the angle at which to stand. The muscles in the foot did not need to be told when and how to act. In fact your ego mind, your 'little voice', was not evident at all, not interfering, not advising, not criticising, not judging, not teaching! Where was it? It had the responsibility of being totally aware of the forces acting on your body. That was sufficiently absorbing and there was no desire to 'interfere'. The body did the responding but the 'little voice' did the monitoring.

Do you see the difference? Our egos *do* have a role to play in our skiing. They monitor all the influences on the body, internal and external. The body adjusts its responses according to the feedback it receives. The problems start when the ego takes over the controls and becomes the performer as well as doing the monitoring.

. . . Or this one

Just like the previous exercise where we stood balanced on a tube train or bus, this time go to the local park or recreation ground. There you may find a roundabout. Stand on it facing forwards, holding onto the rail, while a friend pushes it round. Leave go of the rail and balance on your feet. Get your friend to push faster and then slower. Begin to notice what's happening. Is it an enjoyable experience? Do you feel the involuntary movements in your feet which are keeping you balanced? Compare the weight on your outside foot with that on the inside foot – did you *choose* to make them different? Notice the shape your body is making, and the position of the hips and the knees. This is similar to the position you will be in when you are turning on skis. The lessons you may learn from these experiments are:

- The body will get itself into the appropriate position to do the job *if it is allowed to.*
- The ego or 'little voice' can be kept silent and busy if put to kinesthetically monitoring the situation to enable the body to take appropriate action.
- The body could handle the situation itself and did not need countermanding instructions, advice or criticisms from our ego state!

In these two similar experiments we can see that the 'interference factor' was minimal, and as a result the ensuing performance was effective and enjoyable.

"Isn't it different when I go skiing? I don't have a bar in front of me to grab if I'm about to lose control". This is exactly the point. Because you were able to grab something if you needed to, your element of trust in your body was high. You knew you were safe so you let your body get on with the job, free from worry.

What if there had been no bar there? Then it would have been more difficult to trust the body entirely. You could trust it a little bit but then the voice might start: "This is a bit dangerous, isn't it?" – "Suppose I fall and hurt myself?" – "I'm going to look a bit silly if I overbalance in front of all these people".

Suddenly you would not be allowing your body to do what it feels is appropriate. Suddenly your ego state or 'little voice' has things to do other than monitor what's going on. So, firstly your body is receiving far less feedback and thus has less information to go on, and secondly there are instructions flying around which may be countermanding what the body wants to do naturally.

The same thing happens when we go skiing. We don't have the rail to grab, the trust is reduced and the interferences multiply!

KEEPING THE EGO OCCUPIED

In the next six days we look at how to keep the ego state occupied and effective, doing what it knows how to do best rather than interfering with the naturalness of the body's movements.

A large part of our Ski Skills courses is about recognising the importance of the two functions of 'monitoring' and 'performing' and keeping them separate and independent. The degree to which you can do this is the degree to which you will ski as you've always wanted to.

Our ego cannot be quietened like a noisy child and told to shut up! It needs recognition and appreciation and if you give it neither of these it will constantly interfere. Respect it for the valuable job it does for your skiing; keep it busy and always employed. The body will then have all the facts to make the appropriate actions. NOW THE EGO WILL NEVER INTERFERE!

TRUST AND TECHNIQUE

When you see a skier who looks awkward on the mountain you could say that his awkwardness is due to a lack of technique – simply apply the correct technique and the awkwardness will evaporate. Yes, lack of effective technique *is* being demonstrated, but why? The reason for the awkwardness lies one step in front of the lack of technique. When the skier is reluctant to trust his body to produce the manoeuvre he wants, and he is reluctant to trust his skis to perform as they were designed, awkward movements will follow. The lack of technique is due mainly to the lack of trust that precedes it. It follows that once a skier begins to trust his body and his skis, letting them both 'get on with the job', his movements will begin to flow together and he will begin to look and feel more confident.

What is technique?

What an emotive word this is. It seems that the extent to which you have 'technique' is the extent to which you are able to ski. More lessons, more tips, more advice are all that's needed. Then we'll all be able to ski better!

We can define technique as the movements the skier makes to achieve a desired result. To turn to the left requires technique, as does stopping or side-stepping uphill. Indeed you cannot stand, walk or even get out of bed in the morning without technique. The efficiency and effortlessness with which you do these things is related to the degree you trust your body to produce the technique that achieves the result you want.

How did people learn to ski before there were any ski instructors? They went out and experimented until they *could* ski. Then one skier decided to write a book to help those who couldn't ski. All he had in the way of information was his own experience and that of watching others. Once it was written down it was seen by the reader as 'technique', and skiing then had to be done 'this way'. The technique I would like you to use from now on is *your* technique – the technique that *your* body discovers works best for you.

Stand up, close your eyes and lift one foot off the floor. Be aware of the many muscle movements in the foot supporting your weight. Then transfer your attention to the foot in the air and notice the way it is moving slightly, acting as a balancing weight. Then consider the weighted knee and notice the tension, if any, in that area. It's not a difficult exercise, but to do it requires technique. It helps when the legs are relaxed, but the body, when trusted to do that simple task, will perform very well. The amount of sway of your unweighted leg was 'technique', the amount of flex in the weighted knee was 'technique', the many minute movements in the foot on the floor were 'technique' – and we surely cannot pretend we knew what was going on down there!

Trust produces technique by allowing the body not only to do what it knows how to do, but also to learn what it cannot yet do.

By trying out the 'drills' in this book you will discover a great deal of technique: much of it will be new, and all of it will increase your efficiency and effectiveness as a skier.

If, however, I merely *told* you how to ski in the way that I think is currently in vogue, I would deny you the very learning experiences you need in order to ski well.

Trusting your skis
On the second day of our programme we shall be looking closely at how our skis work. They are superbly crafted instruments designed to turn a moving body with little effort. When we have experienced the effect our skis can produce for us, and learned to trust them the way we trust the steering wheel of a car to turn the wheels, we can stop trying so hard and instead let them get on with the job!

WHAT DO YOU WANT FROM YOUR SKIING?

So far we have looked at learning in general and how we can trust our bodies to perform both familiar and unfamiliar actions. But all of this is of no practical benefit unless we have a sense of direction. Where do we want to take our skiing? What kind of skier do we want to be? What is all this learning for anyway?

Before you began reading this book you may have had very clear ambitions for your skiing. Or you may just be wanting to improve or increase your enjoyment of skiing. What *do* you want from your skiing?

On our Ski Skills course I begin each day by asking my pupils what they want to achieve from their skiing that day. Skiing means different things to everybody, as is emphasised by the variety of their replies:

- "I want to ski as fast as my wife (husband)."
- "I want to ski with more confidence in the bumps."
- "I want to feel the rhythm off-piste."
- "I want to feel relaxed."
- "I want to feel as happy on 'red' runs as I do on 'blue' ones."
- "I'm looking for more control and to overcome my fear of ice."

Making a clear statement of what they want to achieve produces a mental image of the action they want to perform. In their minds' eye they see themselves skiing confidently down moguls, bouncing rhythmically through the powder or skilfully finding a controlled route through an icy piste.

Without that mental picture the objective has no validity, the pupil secretly does not believe it, they know

The extremes of ambition. Patrick Vallencant was a novice once!

it is unrealistic and so discard it. I rarely hear unlikely aims. "Short-listing for an Olympic team place" or "from nursery slopes to the couloirs in one week" are seldom the aspirations of the holiday skier. Their aims are much more readily achievable. Not because their aims are more modest but because they can actually 'see' themselves achieving what they want. They can believe that, all things being equal, they will get there in the time they are allocating themselves to the pursuit of their aims.

In selecting *your* objectives you are taking the SINGLE MOST EFFECTIVE STEP towards success. Nothing in this book will be as powerful to you as the *clarity* with which you identify your objectives, short-term and long-term, and the *commitment with which you pursue them.*

But beware of the implied limitations! Your objective may be to ski a certain challenging run confidently without falling, by the end of the week. The limitation that this puts on our success is the failure to recognise that we may have the potential for a far *greater* improvement in our skiing than merely to the level we have arbitrarily chosen.

Remember the example of the acorn? Its potential to become an oak tree is clear and fundamental. As skiers we do not know the exact potential of our skiing ability, we only trust we have a potential to be fulfilled. As no two oak trees are the same shape or height, so also no two skiers are the same. To pursue blindly an inflexible objective could deny you amazing possibilities of fulfilling your potential in a slightly different direction. The downhill racer with his sight set on winning the Hahnenkamm Race in Kitzbühel may discover in the middle of his ten-year training that his abilities are more suited to Giant Slalom. Instinctively he would change direction and allow his ambition to flow in line with this unfolding potential.

When our pupils decide on a goal they do not know the route they will take to get there. They do not describe the details of each skiing manoeuvre their bodies are going to have to learn. At this stage of the course they will not even have thought about trusting their bodies or their skis! By the end of the week they will have learned a lot about themselves and their skiing. Objectives may have been reached or replaced, achievements established and progress made. Looking back, the path to success will rarely have been a straight one, and success may not be what they thought it was going to be either!

Sometimes a pupil will say to me "I'll just come along to see what it is all about, and see what you can do for me. I'm fairly open to any ideas". Indeed you could well be thinking that as you read this chapter now!

It is understandable to feel reluctant at first to state an objective. For one thing, in choosing to pursue one objective you have to ignore another. There is also the possibility of failing to achieve your objective and letting yourself down in your own eyes and in the eyes of others. How much safer to stand uncommitted on the sidelines watching the action from a distance. There's no risk there! But there is no action either! That only happens when you are in the middle of it – knowing what you want and committed to getting it. Afterwards, when you have had the experience of the action, *then* you can analyse what results you get from the experiment, or the exercise. That would be based on the most valuable thing you can take away from it, your experience of it!

When your objectives conflict

I was once told by a pupil that he wanted to achieve two things that week. He wanted to improve his powder skiing technique, and he wanted never to fall over. It became clear that when he was skiing in the powder he was rigid and stiff, and though never falling over, he was making little progress either. His intention never to fall over was the more dominant. When asked to explain how he was going to achieve his objective of improving in the powder, he realised that skiers in the powder do fall over. When he saw that falling was an inevitable part of learning to ski powder, and that to fall did not mean to fail, he relaxed much more, fell much more, and began to improve very quickly.

COMMITMENT

I've mentioned commitment a few times already and I make no apologies for expanding on it again. Commitment is the vital ingredient in the recipe of learning new skills. If it's not included in generous measure the result can be dissatisfaction, disillusionment and despair.

Commitment is *not* the same as trying! *Trying* is admitting self-doubt. When you are determined to achieve a certain result your ego voice, doubting your ability, may be heard urging you to greater efforts. The greater effort produces bodily tension which interferes with your natural power and ability and a fall is generally not far behind. *Commitment* is being clear about what you want whilst trusting that you have the potential to achieve it. Do you keep your foot on the brake when you are accelerating on the motorway?

You *can* be committed to a number of things in your skiing. You can be committed to skiing the next run as smoothly as you can. You can be committed to achieving from your skiing what you set out to achieve at the beginning of the day or week. You can be committed to expressing the maximum pleasure you can imagine from the next run. You can be committed to doing precisely and exclusively what your coach asks you to do, or indeed you ask yourself to do, as you ski the next stretch of mountain.

Commitment is the result of choice. You don't *have* to chase the objective you've set yourself, you don't *have* to ski the run you're on, you choose to do so! When you choose to do something you are a long way towards doing it with a high level of commitment. When you have a high level of commitment your attention is focussed specifically on what you've chosen to do and on the way you've chosen to do it. This focus leaves little room for extraneous thoughts to enter your consciousness and diffuse your concentration.

Your level of commitment can be mirrored directly by physical changes in your body. Recently, skiing in poor visibility with a group, I noticed how our skiing had deteriorated as conditions worsened. Legs became stiff and turns were ragged. Enjoyment was disappearing fast! We were all allowing the weather to affect our performance.

With visibility down to 10 metres I stopped the group on a run I know well. "How would we ski this run if we could all see the piste ahead perfectly?" I asked them. "Can you show me over the next hundred metres?" "Well, I wouldn't be skiing like this", said one member, "I'd be skiing the fall line!" And he took off into the fog on a direct line producing remarkable shortswings. The rest of the group followed, immediately recovering their old form. Suddenly it was fun again, we discovered we could see more than we thought we could, and we were much

TRY ANOTHER EXERCISE

It doesn't seem to be working

Occasionally a pupil will say in frustration, "It's not working!" – "I'm getting nothing out of this" – even "I'm bored"!

The whole 'Inner Skiing' approach to learning depends on feedback; the feedback to yourself, from yourself, about what you are doing. Negative feedback is just as valuable as positive. Feedback is only of any value if it is the truth. Then you will have a clear position from which to proceed.

LOOKING FOR RESULTS

If you do an experiment having already decided upon the result you are looking for, there is little value in doing it. If you are trying to arrive at a set result you are excluding all the learning potential of the exercise.

Many skiers have very fixed ideas on how they *should* look, or how they *should* feel. Consequently they try to make every exercise or experiment, which is designed to increase their learning, fit the result they want. Sadly it doesn't work that way! You will see the 'results' all over the mountain with awkward, contorted body positions everywhere. The result is not always the point of an exercise. The value and the learning are in the doing!

For example, a class of six pupils experimenting with an exercise to notice their breathing and the way it changes while they ski, will almost certainly report six different results. All will be valuable because what they are reporting is what is true for them! If instead I had said, "As you turn I want you to inhale at the beginning of the turn and exhale slowly throughout" I would be giving them a result.

When you are skiing in a fairly relaxed fashion, the breathing often forms a pattern which harmonizes with the turning of the skis. This harmony contributes to the flowing effect of the movement of 'good' skiers. For each of us our breathing will harmonize in different ways at different times.

The value of this exercise is to recognise that there may be a connection between our breathing pattern and our skiing. The point is *not* to try and duplicate my breathing pattern or what somebody else says is the right pattern, but for you to recognise your own pattern.

more relaxed. A hundred metres? We forgot to stop! We were committed to our skiing – that was all that had been missing.

Later, when I asked them what physical differences they had felt at the start of the exercise, they replied:

"My head lifted up as I looked further ahead."

"My weight moved forward off my heels."

"My arms reached forward."

"My knees and ankles flexed in anticipation."

These differences were entirely the result of increased commitment.

Every one of the games, drills and exercises in this book you can do already. They are not difficult. Their value for you lies mainly in the commitment you have when you do them. Choose one yourself and your commitment to it will be high; the value is then in the doing, and the learning is in the awareness of what is happening to your skis, or your body, as you are doing it. The breakthroughs will happen when your commitment to an exercise is at a level of 95 to 100 per cent. Below 80 per cent you are practically wasting your time. When your commitment is low, the value is low. Choose to raise your commitment or try another exercise. Either will be immensely more beneficial!

Once you have recognised it you will also quickly notice when the pattern changes. This could be from anxiety, a change in terrain or a sudden unexpected manoeuvre, and there will be learning from recognising these changes. Later we might play a game of 'skiing while breathing to a pattern we choose' and keeping it rhythmic whatever outside influences try to change it. This will produce more learning and more results, again different ones for different people. The breathing will always interrupt its rhythm if the body is being *made* to do something as opposed to being *allowed* to do something.

This experiment can therefore give us instant feedback about when that is happening. Imagine what you would be missing if you thought that the idea was merely to reproduce an instruction. I'd be bored, too, after thirty seconds!

So when you look for results and become attached to them, you are diminishing the value of the exercise.

RELAXED CONCENTRATION

Whenever you watch an athlete or an artist performing at the highest level of their skill they generally express qualities that lift them out of the mass of those who perform the same movements but at a lower standard. See a tennis player, an ice skater, a ballet dancer or a skier, particularly a slalom specialist, at the top of their professions. Whenever I see great performances I am always struck by their relaxed appearance. No strained facial muscles nor gritted teeth. No awkward movements, no hurry. No wonder we so often hear "They make it all seem so easy!" This almost hypnotic state of relaxation is achieved through concentration – and when

concentration' as Timothy Gallwey and Bob Kriegel describe the state in their book *Inner Skiing*, is the master skill because this is the time when our potential is given full rein. This is the time when breakthroughs happen, when times are improved upon, when performances are bettered. This is the time when the enjoyment and satisfaction of the experience are at their peak. We've all had some insight into this state already. In skiing it may have been the best run you did all holiday which left you speechless with pleasure. There is no element of 'trying' in this state, just 'being', and once you've experienced it, if only for a few seconds, you are constantly searching to re-create it, and live it again.

Relaxation and concentration are harder to achieve the more you strive for them. Throughout this book everything we shall be doing together will help us experience this master skill more often.

There are three conditions which are always essential for 'relaxed concentration'; it may help to look at them briefly so we can recognise them later – or recognise their absence! We have discussed them already – but it's when the three fuse together the miracles happen!

● **Commitment** – 100 per cent commitment – to some definite objective.

● **Awareness** – the monitoring of everything the body is doing and the influences it is being subjected to. Beware the introduction of judgement or criticism, or any 'ego' or 'small voice' interference: you'll know then that the feedback function is working at reduced efficiency.

● **Trust** – in yourself and your body to do the tasks you ask of it without having to explain the mechanics! *Trust* that you have the potential to learn what you don't already know. *Trust* that when you are clear about what you want and your awareness is total you cannot help but arrive where you want to go.

The degree to which these elements are present is the degree to which a state of 'relaxed concentration' can be attained.

These conditions are the three cornerstones of the 'Inner Game' approach to learning, and are applicable to any sport. They can revolutionise your skiing where conventional instruction may have failed you again and again. It works!

concentration is that focussed the whole body seems to be quietened and is just left to work at its maximum efficiency.

Relaxation through concentration or 'relaxed

First Day

The first day of a ski holiday is always exciting. For most people it is the first time on skis for a year at least. The objectives of our first day's skiing are:
- to find your ski legs again;
- to begin to experience the 'Ski Skills' approach which will give you confidence and the trust that it will work for you.

Twenty years ago one skier in ten came home with a broken leg. Now it is one in three hundred, and it is becoming safer all the time. Boots and bindings have made an enormous contribution to this improvement. However there are still many unnecessary accidents, and they often occur on the first day. There will not be many instructions in this book, but two of them are right here!

1 **Check your bindings**
2 **Stretch your muscles before straining them.**

CHECK YOUR SAFETY BINDINGS

I am amazed at how often I see skiers on the first day of their holiday leap into their skis, either hired ones or their own, and start skiing, blindly relying on their bindings to release them if they fall.

There is much debate as to whose responsibility it is that bindings are correctly set, and indeed even what is meant by a 'correct' setting. Though ski shops and other professionals may advise and guide you I always recommend that before you start your first run you actually test your own bindings and feel them release you under pressure. The commonest accidents where bindings are blamed are:
- Hired skis with the bindings still set for the previous user.
- Privately owned skis not checked since the previous season.

Get to know how your bindings work even if you prefer a shop to adjust them. Remember to carry with you a screwdriver or suitable tool so that you can carry out emergency adjustments on the mountain.

How to test your bindings

With your ski on the snow, tip against something solid, get a companion to stand on the back of your ski to keep it rigid. Now try to step out of your binding. Repeat it once or twice and you'll feel the degree of pressure on your leg before the release functions and you can decide if adjustment is needed.

For the toe release your companion can gently tap at the side of your toes with their boot. You'll feel and see the toe-piece swivelling outwards before returning to a central point, which will show you that the mechanism is at least working. The adjustment you decide on is up to you, but I prefer to err on the side of safety and start with them on a light setting which can be tightened later if necessary. The other way round is not really recommended!

Remember! The only person responsible for your bindings is you. You cannot delegate that responsibility to your instructor or the ski shop. They will not accept it, and their insurance companies certainly won't!

Be very wary of adjusting anybody else's binding unless they are a member of your own family. There could be a come-back if you get it wrong.

This explains why no one will readily move your binding settings. **Do learn to do it yourself, and know how to check them. Then check them every time you go skiing, and at least once a week.**

If you are worried about adjusting them yourself ask

your ski shop to do it for you. But *always* do the checking yourself.

STRETCHING BEFORE STRAINING

In skiing you use many muscles which rarely get exercised for the rest of the year. If you suddenly put these muscles under great strain without warming them up first they can 'snap'.

Try it with a balloon!

You can compare using your muscles to blowing up a balloon. Try blowing up a balloon without any preparation. Then take another balloon and warm it by holding it in your clenched hand; gently start to stretch it in all directions. Don't force it if it doesn't want to go but

THE HAMSTRING STRETCHER

1 Swing one ski forward so it is standing vertically resting on its heel.
2 Try and push the heel into the ground.
3 Lower your forehead towards your extended knee, reaching as far as you can without strain, hold it for a count of 10 seconds, then relax it again.
4 Repeat with other leg.
5 Repeat exercise five times.

CORPS DE BALLET

1 Place one ski behind you at right angles to the other to form a 'T'.
2 Facing forwards slide the other ski forwards and backwards on as long a track as you can manage.
3 Now face sideways, towards your other ski and repeat the sliding movement. That will find some new muscles!
4 Repeat that with the other ski at the back.
5 Repeat exercise five times.

LET YOUR FINGERS DO THE WALKING!

1 Reach down and touch your toes.
2 Slowly 'walk' your fingers along the front of the skis all the way to the tips (the show-offs go a lot further!)
3 Hold that position for the count of 10.
4 Slowly 'walk' back and stand up.

THE ROLLER COASTER

1 Let the head hang forward so that the chin is touching the chest.
2 Slowly revolve the head around in a full circle gently stretching the muscles in the neck.
3 Then include the shoulders in the circular motion.
4 Now extend the movement so as to rotate at the waist.
A very relaxing exercise – you may hear some strange clicks while you are doing it.

ease it into new stretched shapes. Now blow it up! Wasn't that a lot easier?

The muscles in the body work on the same principles. Warmed up and gently stretched, they are pliable and strong; cold and unused, they are sluggish with a low breaking strain.

By warming up and stretching you should avoid the annoying aches and pains, and particularly the 'pulled' and strained muscles, which many skiers experience in the first few days.

Here are some of my favourite exercises which I do with my group when we meet in the morning. By this time we'll have our skis on which increases the effectiveness of the stretching. I know you can't wait to go skiing again – but fifteen minutes at the beginning of each day in warming up will repay itself many times over.

THE SWINGER

1 Bring your hands up in front of your chest, palms downwards, fingertips touching and both thumbs against the chest.
2 Swing one arm out in a wide arc and follow it through as far as it will go behind you. Notice the place on the horizon the forefinger is pointing to.
3 Repeat the exercise with the other arm.
4 Repeat frequently on both sides seeing if you can swing further round at the end of each arc. I am always amazed at the extra reach we can manage after a few 'goes'.

THE KILLER!

1 With skis about a foot apart raise both hands high above the head.
2 Place your right hand behind the heel of your left boot. It doesn't matter bending your knee for this one!
3 Bring it back up to above your head and repeat with the other hand. Do this exercise in your own time. I like to do it quite fast, others feel they benefit more at a slower rate.
4 Begin to notice where your eyes are looking. See if you can keep your eyes horizontal throughout.
5 Begin to feel the shape which your body naturally adopts for this exercise. A lot of muscles in our trunk which we use for skiing are being stretched in this one!

These are just six warming-up exercises, there are many more. Get into the habit of running through a few at the beginning of each day.

RELAXED MODE AND STRETCHED MODE

One person's relaxed mode is another's stretched mode! On the slopes a run which you felt was stretching your abilities last year may well be easily within your capabilities this year. Recognise the mode you have chosen to ski in. How you feel about your skiing could have more to do with the mode you are skiing in than with your actual abilities.

In a relaxed mode

1 You are skiing well within your level of confidence.
2 Interference from external sources e.g. steepness, fear, other skiers, snow conditions, is reduced to insignificance.
3 Feedback from the body and the skis is at its most informative and accurate.
4 Experimentation is more valuable because there are fewer variable influences.
5 You are able to focus in on any aspect of your skiing.
6 You can discover the aesthetic pleasures of skiing such as rhythm, harmony of movement, balance and 'smoothness'.

In a stretched mode

In a stretched mode these factors are very different. There you encounter thrill, speed, risk, self-doubt, exhilaration – even fear.

In the relaxed mode the body quickly feels what works and what doesn't work. In the stretched mode zone the learning is more random and less focussed.

The focus is not so clear because of all the other interferences. You may be in a stretched mode because of your perception of the terrain, the snow conditions and the speed at which you are skiing it. It is not the slope's fault! You may see other skiers skiing it without a care in the world. Indeed, after you've skied it a few times what started as a stretched mode may become a very relaxed one.

So it is *us* and our attitudes which create 'relaxed modes' and 'stretched modes'.

Begin to recognise the 'mode' you are choosing to be in by the clarity with which you can focus your attention on any single action, be it a part of your body or a point on the horizon. The more your attention is focussed, the closer you are to a 'relaxed mode'.

There is learning in both modes and fun in both modes, and satisfaction in creating relaxed modes from stretched modes. You can see the progress you are making as you go along.

Panic mode

This begins as a 'stretched mode' until suddenly you ski around a corner and. . .

THIS IS YOUR BOOK. HOW WILL YOU USE IT?

All the drills, exercises and games in this book have many things in common. Let's see now what we are really looking for in these drills so it will save time and explanations when we are out there doing them!

1 Every 'drill' is *your* drill. You can choose to do it and you can choose the commitment with which you do it. The learning resulting from it is yours too!

2 Beware of 'looking for a result' (see page 20). Whilst you may get some benefits it will certainly block off a lot more.

3 Get used to making your own 'scale' and then exploring the full range of that scale to find out what happens at each point on it. For example, when varying the weight on your outside ski decide on your scale of 'feel' from *no* weight on that ski through to *all* your weight on that ski. Stand still and check the feel of various positions along that scale, before taking off and testing how they affect your turns.

4 Look for 'what is' before looking for 'what if'. In other words let the exercise tell you what you are doing 'right now' with your skiing. Then explore the whole range of variables in the exercise to find out 'what if'.

5 You cannot fail in any of these drills. There is no pass-mark or standard. The learning comes from the doing.

6 Try to start off in a 'relaxed mode' and then progress to the 'stretched mode' by doing the same drills on increasingly challenging terrain.

7 Every drill and exercise has a purpose: to learn. There are often other purposes too. Some are obvious, others are less so. Sometimes I will describe the purposes but often I will not, for knowing the purpose may cause you to anticipate the result rather than learn from the experience. You won't improve your skiing from just reading this book! You have to get out there and 'discover' for yourself. Then the purpose may be obvious!

8 Reporting the findings. Every drill and exercise gives you an experience that is unique to you. What was *your* experience of the drill? What were *your* findings? What was *your* learning?

READY TO GO SKIING?

Are we all set? Have you got everything:
- lift-pass?
- gloves?
- hat?
- goggles?
- sunglasses?
- suntan cream?
- money?

Right, let's go! Here are some drills for getting back on skis.

LOOKING AROUND YOU

1 Choose a 'comfortable' slope.

2 Imagine you are a tourist on a sightseeing trip. On this first run pretend you will never be repeating this exact ski run again and at the bottom you will have to describe everything you saw around you as you skied down.

3 If you are with a companion point out, with your finger, the things that catch your eye: a ski-lift pylon, a numbered piste-marker, a moving car below, a rocky outcrop, an aeroplane above.

4 Compare some of the things you saw with your companions. Try to spot something which you think the others may have missed!

The purpose of the drill:

- It's your first run, maybe in a strange resort, so notice where you are. Pick out the strange things in this new environment. Enjoy the scenery. Appreciate the difference between your normal environment back home and where you are now.

- Your body is being trusted to ski. It could do it last year, and though it may feel strange at first it hasn't forgotten completely!

- Forget about 'skiing well'! There's plenty of time to worry about that, if you insist!

- Realise that there are no rules as to where you *should* look when you ski. So look ahead, above you, below you, everywhere!

CHECK OUT YOUR BODY

Your body is going to be very active this week, constantly moving, stretching, absorbing, bending. So let's just check out the body, see if it is all there and that everything is working. If it's not working, reassure yourself that at least it's still there!

On this next run focus your attention on as many moving parts in your body as you can find while you ski.

1 Start with the toes! Move them around, bend them and wriggle them, scrunch them up, then release them. Working OK?

2 Next the ankle; bend it right forwards and then backwards several times. A spot of oil needed there?

3 Flex the calf muscles as tight as they can go. They already *are* as tight as they can go? What would if feel like if they were loose?

4 Now to the knees. Check the complete range of bend from straight up and down to totally bent. Wiggle them sideways, flapping like someone who has just seen a ghost! Plenty of movement in those knees, isn't there?

5 A flex or two of the thigh muscles and then on to the bottom. Tighten all those muscles and then let them go.

6 The waist next. Bend forward as far as you can and then straighten up like a toy soldier. Then turn at the waist as far right and as far left as you can.

7 Rotate the shoulder and the elbows making sure all those joints work. Move the arms around like windmills.

8 Clench and release the fingers. Then clench and release the toes at the same time as the fingers. All of them working?

9 Move the head around, letting it roll around the shoulders.

10 Finally check out the vision by looking in every direction around you. Don't leave any angle out – backwards through your legs too!

Every muscle and joint we've located you will be needing and using. When we know they are there and do work (to a greater or lesser extent!), we can begin to trust them to get on with the job.

Any discoveries you make during this body check are valuable. Any tension anywhere? At this stage just notice and be aware of it.

How has your skiing been during all this? We have not been concentrating on it, so how has it been getting on, on its own?

SKATING

1 On flat ground, perhaps near the bottom of the run, before you go up the lift, have a skate around. From one ski push off onto the other as if on ice-skates. Enjoy the sensation of sliding on one ski before letting it push you off on to the other ski in another direction.

2 See if you can complete large circles, clockwise and anti-clockwise.

3 Imagine yourself skating on a village pond. Let the arms swing to provide impetus and balance. Begin to feel what's happening in your feet. Notice the pressures at the front of the foot, and then the heel.

4 Notice your knees and your ankles. How flexible are you letting them be?

5 Feel your body adapting to a new environment and a slippery surface. To let the body find its balance, try skating in an upright elegant way like a soldier on parade. Then try skating as a long-jump athlete might sprint towards the take-off mark. Somewhere in between those extremes your body will discover a balanced position that feels comfortable.

6 If you can't get to grips with skating on skis, it doesn't matter! Something is blocking the freedom of movement and we shall discover it later in some other exercise. Then you can skate later in the week and see the difference.

7 If you skated successfully you will have:
- stretched a few muscles;
- felt the result of a coordinated independent leg action;
- tired yourself out!

YOUR FOOT IS AS LONG AS YOUR SKI

An early exercise for us in visualisation (we'll do more on Day 6).

1 Pretend your foot is as long as your ski. Your toes are reaching out as far as the turned-up part of your skis, and your heel is stretched out behind you at the back – like a circus clown with those enormous boots!

2 Feel the contours of the ground under your new feet. Quite easy, when they are almost two metres long!

3 If you can't feel anything through your new feet slow right down until you can.

4 Let the feet begin to 'read' the terrain by feel rather than relying on input through your eyes.

5 What do you experience from this exercise? Just the same? More control? More or less balance?

GET THAT BIG TOE FEELING!

As we walk or run, our toes, especially our big toes, play an important part in keeping us balanced.

1 Focus your attention on the big toe and see what it is doing to balance you as you ski. Ask yourself these questions:

"How much of my weight is on it?"

"At what stage of the turn do I first feel it?"

"Is the big toe of my outside foot on one turn more weighted than the big toe on the opposite foot on the next turn?"

2 Sometimes I hear my group calling out "big toe", "big toe", "big toe" when each big toe in turn helps to absorb the pressures of the turn. They are reminded of the important part the big toe plays in our skiing. But don't make a rule up now, like "I must put all my weight on my big toe!" Just notice what your big toe is doing and see if you are allowing it to make its contribution.

3 There is a lot of value in this exercise in a 'stretched mode', on some steep bumps for example. The steeper the better!

4 What effect do you notice from this awareness of the big toe? How has it affected your skiing? Remember you don't have to be able to theorise a result in order to repeat it. The learning has been picked up by the body anyway.

Here's a couple of 'imaging' games I like to play with a group on the first day. Skiers can be so worried about their skiing that their attention is all on judging their performance and not on simply enjoying being back on skis again. After a year of running a home or working in an office one of the hardest things to do on the slopes, on the first day, is 'letting go'! Letting go of searching for control, letting go of judging your performance, letting go of your 'act' which sees you through the other fifty weeks a year. When we pretend, for fun, to be something other than a skier struggling down a slope, we can discover qualities that we weren't allowing ourselves to express.

THE RAG DOLL

How would you ski if you were a rag doll?

1 Just stand on your skis, collapse like a rag doll, and feel this strange body position. Do you feel your boots virtually propping you up?

2 Ski the next slope, floppily, rag-doll style. Don't forget (though this may seem strange), not every game we will play is directly aimed at improving your skiing. No good skier is bent virtually double, arms dangling and poles trailing – but can you pick up qualities which you don't detect in your own skiing? How is your balance? Where is your weight on your feet? Are your shoulders feeling relaxed? Were you trusting your body and skis to get on with the skiing?

3 If you like the 'rag-doll' feeling and you were being one 100 per cent, ski the next run at 80 per cent. Have you retained the rag-doll qualities whilst now feeling a little more like a 'normal' skier?

THE MOTOR BIKE

1 Choose the imaginary motor bike you'd like to ride. Notice your choice – is this really how you see yourself? The selection can range from a small 50cc 'putt-putt' with a shopping basket on the front to a massive 1000cc job!

2 On this next run, sit astride your bike, reach for the handlebars, check out the controls, turn on the headlights, kick the starter and take off.

3 Are you sitting comfortably in the saddle? How responsive is your steering of the handlebars? Can you weave around the moguls and take it anywhere you want to go?

4 Are you revving up and accelerating out of the corners and changing gear to go into them? Now's the chance to make the "BRRRM BRRRM" noises which are obligatory on a motor bike, especially one on a ski slope!

5 As you get more into this game and you *become* the motor bike so your 'skier' gets left behind. In our classes we race on our bikes, play 'cops and robbers' and ride in formations. Others around us may think we're mad but some of us will have never skied so fast, nor felt so secure ever before! When the going gets tough, reach for the handlebars, rev up the throttle and get going. You'll cruise down anything!

CHUCK IT IN THE CIRCLE!

We are going to spend the week concentrating on the feedback our bodies and skis are giving us – often very subtle nuances of information that, if we can pick them up, will tell us all we need to know about our skiing. Will you be able to focus in with a high level of concentration if:

- You've just received a phone call from your office telling you a big account is threatening to leave.
- You've just had a row with your husband/wife.
- The weather has closed in and you feel you can't see a thing!
- The powder snow you were expecting has turned to crust.
- You have a hangover and you think you shouldn't have got out of bed.
- You can't remember whether you cancelled the milk deliveries back home before you left!
- You expected to be skiing in a group of higher/lower standard.

Any one of these thoughts will be blocking some of the feedback and getting in the way. They are not wanted at the moment although they all have to be dealt with eventually.

You have three clear choices:

1 Deal with the matter *now* before you go out on the slopes.

2 Decide to deal with it after your day's skiing.

3 Carry it around in your mind all day so you can keep referring to it as you ski!

Which do you prefer?

I always ask my group if they have any matters which might interfere with their enjoyment of the day. Mostly they are mentally prepared for the day's skiing but a few do volunteer some problems!

If they need to make an urgent telephone call I suggest they make it now and rejoin us later.

If they are disappointed with the conditions I suggest they accept the conditions are what they are and not the conditions they'd like. Recognising the difference, they can choose to ski in these conditions or not! It's amazing how your attitude to the conditions affects your behaviour. When you *choose* to ski in bad light it is never as 'bad' as when you ski in it wishing it was sunny!

If they've had a row they can decide to go back and settle matters now, or wait to do that after the skiing.

In fact whatever the worry or thought that might spoil your enjoyment, it's no good keeping it in the forefront of your mind.

There is one special way of getting rid of all distractions – and it works practically every time.

I draw a circle in the snow in front of the group with my ski stick. I then invite anyone who is anxious, concerned, worried, distracted, or disappointed at *anything* to state the distraction, and by stabbing at the circle with their ski stick, leave it behind! I tell them all that at the end of the class we can come by and pick it up again. I always do make a point of checking with them if they want to deal with the matter at the end. Usually it has become irrelevant, often it has been forgotten, but if it is a matter that needs attention it can be handled at this point without having interfered with the day's skiing. The next time you have a distraction deal with it there and then or 'chuck it in the circle'!

Such a suggestion may seem over-simple when you read it here. But I've seen greater improvement in a pupil's skiing after performing this one action than in a whole week concentrating on their skiing if there has been something on their mind.

If in playing these two games you managed to forget it is your first day back on skis you've achieved a great deal. You have also begun to appreciate the amazing potential for learning which imagery can give you.

So you've found your 'ski legs' again. Now where do we go from here? You can go anywhere you want when you know where you are!

YOUR OBJECTIVE FOR THE WEEK

What do you want to have achieved in your skiing after using this book? Only *you* will know – but the choice is endless: more enjoyment, more confidence, relaxation, a new technique, a faster time perhaps.

Decide on a time limit for getting where you want to be: a week, two days, an afternoon, an hour?

Stating a time is *really* taking responsibility for achieving what you want. Notice how your choice of time is a 'reasonable' one. It is rare to hear anyone being absurdly ambitious.

Beginners often look up to the top of the mountain and say "In two weeks I want to ski from up there". They don't say "By this afternoon I'd like to ski from up there"! Two weeks is enough of a challenge to them, but it is an objective they feel they could reach. It is probably the very limit of their vision, the ultimate achievement. For

you, if you can state your objective and see yourself achieving it, you *will* achieve it. A bold statement? I see the evidence daily, but don't take my word for it. It will work for you too.

When you are clear what you want, see if you can break your objective down into 'bite-sized chunks'! An experienced skier might choose as his aim to ski powder snow making short swing turns from top to bottom. If his experience so far is that after only two turns he always falls, choosing to do a hundred or so linked turns might seem an impossible challenge. So why not, for the first day, make five linked turns the goal? Next day ten and the following day twenty. Don't these seem easier to achieve? With success comes more success, and the 'hundred' will just be another step along the way.

When I'm standing on top of a mogul slope with a pupil who can't believe how far it is to the bottom I always suggest they look for the first three turns. That seems easy! We do those three and then we look at the next five. The next section might be seven, and from there the rest looks straightforward. What seemed horrendous from the top has been tamed by 'breaking it down'.

Break up your 'big' objective into hourly or daily chunks. You'll see the progress continually, and you can check your position with your final goal as you go along.

SKIING AS A QUESTION

This book, and the Ski Skills approach, is not about answers, or solutions. It's not about fads, gimmicks, fashions, instructions, tricks, advice or tips. For those looking for the answers that all these things suggest I have to say you will be disappointed.

Learning is in the question: the questions you ask yourself, or your coach asks you, or I ask you in this book. It is the process of finding an answer to these questions which produces the learning and creates the value, not necessarily the answer itself. This process can take place at a conscious or subconscious level, or both. For example, if I ask a pupil "Whereabouts on your outside foot is your weight concentrated during a run?" the process of determining an answer requires extremely focussed attention on just one of the many complex features which make up a manoeuvre on skis. On a conscious level there is value, and hence learning, in the pupil just being aware of where the weight is. On a

34

subconscious level the body is discovering the effects on itself of its own weight distribution and how that can vary.

The answer may not be accurate – who can judge its accuracy anyway? The answer is certainly neither right nor wrong. But the pursuit of an answer generates a process which will, in itself, produce the learning, achieve your objective and allow the optimum development of your potential.

We live in a world where 'ready answers' are easy to get. Like 'convenience food' they are instant and easily digested and give immediate, but rarely long-lasting satisfaction.

The value, the nourishment, the 'goodness', like roughage in a diet, is not convenient. It needs preparation, discrimination and dedication but when digested has infinitely more beneficial and permanent effect. In skiing the value in learning comes from the process of discovering answers to the questions you ask.

This book will help you ask those questions and will guide you through the process of finding the answers.

SUMMING UP THE FIRST DAY'S SKIING

Don't expect miracles on the first day! You have been presented with some radically new ideas and concepts; let their values unfold during the week as you try out the games and drills I'll be suggesting.

Don't be concerned with understanding what may seem an unfamiliar approach. The learning will come from experience, and not from theoretical analysis.

By now you will be used to being on skis again and will feel more familiar in this new environment – and that's the main point of the day!

Use the space at the end of each day to make your own notes: what worked for you, what didn't work, and anything you want to remember for your next day's skiing.

_____

_____

_____

_____

_____

_____

_____

_____

_____

_____

_____

_____

_____

Second Day

Today we are going to have a look at our skis and discover how they have been designed to make turning very easy – if we can only leave them to perform without our interfering.

We have a part to play too, and when we trust our body to work *with* our skis instead of *against* them, efficiency and smoothness is the result.

The last twenty years have seen a revolution in ski design. My first pair of skis (in 1961) were made of laminated wood with screw-in metal edges. And they were very, very long! Especially for a poor beginner. When I raised my hand above my head with my ski up-ended beside me the tip of the ski would reach to my wrist.

Why were they so long? Because if they were shorter they wouldn't have taken the pressure of my weight and they might have broken. Indeed they often did anyway.

These monsters had to be turned! All our efforts, all our instructors' advice, all our practice was aimed at turning those skis as efficiently as possible.

Look at skiers on the mountain today. Most of them are still working at 'turning those skis'. You can see it from the way they twist and turn their bodies and swing their shoulders from side to side. It is as if skiing is a problem to be solved and the problem is 'How to get the ski to turn me?'

LET'S EXAMINE OUR SKIS

1 Pick up a ski and look at it as if you'd never seen one before. Look along its length by squinting along it from the tip to the base. Do you notice its beautiful curves, the widest part at the toe and the heel and the thinnest around the middle. As graceful as an hour-glass!

2 Now put your skis on and stand comfortably on a flattened slope keeping your weight on your uphill ski. Place the lower ski on the snow beside you resting it lightly on its inside edge. Let your ski poles balance you.

3 With no weight on this lower ski it is being supported only at the toe and the heel. Can you see daylight underneath your foot? If not, is the slope flat or have you got any weight on that ski? Do you notice the upward curve or camber of the ski which when rested weightless on its edge leaves the section of ski under your foot clear of the ground by at least a centimetre?

4 What happens when you now put your weight on the lower ski without changing its position? The daylight has

36

gone, the whole ski edge from top to bottom is touching the snow and the ski has just demonstrated its most amazing capacity to change shape!

Now the camber of the ski is reversed. Do you see the arc that it has made for you? One beautiful sweeping curve all along one edge – this is the curve along which we will ski. The ski manufacturer has designed your ski to produce that arc itself. Our job is merely to stay on the ski and enjoy the ride along the track that the arc will make!

TRUSTING YOUR OUTSIDE SKI

As you ski – and it doesn't matter what standard you are – become aware of the track of your outside ski on each turn. Notice when the track starts and follow it through all the way until the other ski takes over.

Are you trusting it? Are you letting it complete its natural arc, or are you interfering with it halfway around? You can tell the difference very easily. If you are not interfering but simply letting the ski ride its own arc, each turn will be flowing, uniform and unhurried all the way through to its completion.

To achieve this you really have to trust your skis. Halfway into your turn there is a moment when you are

Your ski as a bow

facing right down the fall line. "UGH! I don't like this" skiers say to themselves. They immediately override their automatic pilot and forcibly manoeuvre their skis out of the fall line into the next traverse. "Phew!" they say, "I only feel safe when I'm traversing, I'll get those wretched turns over as fast as I can!"

And that's what you see most skiers on the mountain doing: a series of traverses interrupted by hurried, jagged turns. Discover the joy of the turn and you will discover the joy of skiing. And the joy of turning only reveals itself when you totally trust that outside ski to keep its arc and take you along for the ride.

You can easily tell if a skier is not trusting the ski in a turn. See if you can recognise these:

- Twisting the heels of the ski to change direction, scraping the backs of the skis around.
- Exaggerated planting of the pole right up at the tip of the ski, so all the weight is at the front of the ski.
- Hurriedly placing the inside ski next to the outside one halfway through the turn in case anyone sees that for a split second your skis are not parallel!
- A strained upper body being used by the skier to initiate the turn and control the skis.

The symptoms of not trusting your skis are always the same. The arc of your track through the turn is not uniform or smooth; it will be broken, jagged and hurried.

Let the skis be the vehicle of the turn and you – the skier – be the passenger. Don't take over the driving seat halfway through the turn!

Be aware of your ski track

1 Focus your attention on the track of your outside ski. Notice the exact line it is making. Are you interfering with it or is it a smooth curve?

2 As most skiers hurry through their turns, ask yourself "How would it be if I had much more time to make the turn?"

3 Let the arcs you are now making be twice the radius. Do you see a difference in your turns?

4 Let the game you are playing be 'letting the ski make uniform arcs' and not 'skiing properly'. The first one can be fun and rewarding. The second is far too difficult and rarely successful!

5 There are four ways to notice the track your ski is making:

- *Feeling* an increase in tension in your body at any point through the turn.
- *Looking* behind you to see the track in the snow.
- *Hearing* the smoothness of the sound of your ski throughout the turn; and
- *Asking a friend* to report back what they see!

6 Our skis are designed to turn. I want you to discover the best technique for letting them do so. By constantly monitoring what they are doing you will be making subtle changes in your technique to produce the result you want – a smooth uniform curve. You will also be noticing when your 'technique' is getting in the way of the natural flow of the turn.

7 Don't worry about what your inside ski is doing! Is your aim to discover 'efficient' skiing, totally trusting the effectiveness of that outside ski, or is it to keep your skis together and parallel at all times?

This exercise is about trust, letting go of 'trying' and increasing your awareness of what's going on. I trust that when you are really aware of the line your skis are taking, the intricate technique required to produce the line you want will follow as a result of this awareness. Try it and see!

Where should the weight be on my ski?

Whenever I ask pupils to ski just feeling where their weight is on their foot, and ultimately on their ski, they often ask me "Where *should* my weight be?" The answer is, "There is no best place"!

I cannot tell you how to balance, but I can suggest you feel for yourself where the body wants to balance. Many skiers have been told they must have their weight forward, or in a certain position, to ski effectively. Their attention is focussed in trying to get their weight in what they understand to be the 'best place', instead of discovering the place for themselves. You'll understand what I mean if you try standing on one leg on the ground without skis on; there is no 'best place' for your weight to be on the foot you are standing on, but you soon discover what is not appropriate!

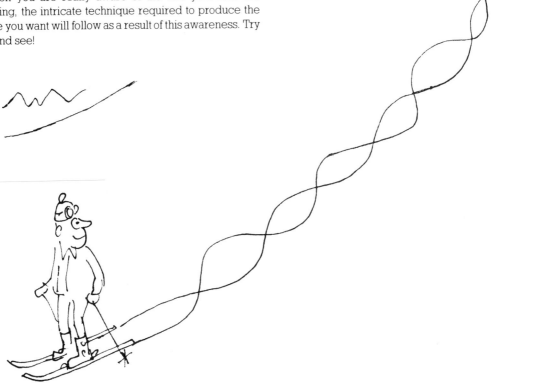

FEELING THE WEIGHT ON YOUR SKI

1 Stand across the slope and lift up your top ski, balancing on the lower one.

2 Feel where the weight is spread on the balancing foot. Is it forward, back, in the middle, spread over the whole foot or along one side? Do you feel many small corrections being made to keep you balanced? Can you identify the balance point, and do you notice that the little corrections mean you are rarely *on* the balance point but rather constantly oscillating around it?

3 Now ski, looking and feeling for this same balance point as you move and turn. It is going to be in the same place, but the range of movement about this point will vary much more.

When you are focussed in on the point at where your weight naturally wants to be and you trust the movement around this point, it is then OK to have the weight where it is – forward, back, in the middle; wherever!

YOUR SKI AS A BOW

Even if you've never shot a bow and arrow in your life, if you picked up a bow and held it one hand in the aiming position you would instinctively hold it in the middle. Either side of the mid-point would result in the arrow aiming wildly above or below where you wanted it to go. Holding it in the middle would feel 'right'.

Your skis have been designed like a bow. They are at their most effective when they are handled like one. The best arc for the ski to follow around the turn is the symmetrical one.

1 As you ski imagine your weight on the outside ski is making a bow of that ski. Now, where is the weight on your foot?

2 Change the tension in the bow on each turn. Really stretch that bow on some turns and let it be slacker on others. Do you feel the difference? How does that change the arc of your turns?

3 The more clearly you can imagine your ski as a bow, the more effective this exercise will be. This is true, of course, of all the exercises that require you to use your imagination!

How much do you trust your skis?

If you want to achieve smooth and effortless skiing, this is a question you will need to ask yourself. The arc your skis make during the turn will help you answer the question.

To build up trust, do these exercises on a simple slope first where you have space and safety in which to experiment. Compare left turns with right turns and consider the differences. On one turn you may well be trusting the ski more than on the other. The difference will be tension somewhere in your leg or body. The next exercise may help you locate it.

Beginning the turn

If you took off one of your skis and 'scooted' it across the slope without its safety stoppers on, within a few metres it would begin to turn downhill and find its own way straight down the slope. Gravity is on your side at the beginning of a turn!

Try it for yourself by skiing with your skis slightly apart on a traverse, then standing up with no pressure or tension in your body and with your skis perfectly flat. You will find that they will slowly start to turn downhill of their own accord. If they don't, maybe you are doing something to interfere with the natural pull of gravity.

So your skis *can* turn with no positive initiation at all. But we can't usually wait for gravity to initiate the turn, so it has to come from us!

The following game, 'Which part of your body leads into the turn?', is an exercise both in *awareness* and in *feedback* of exactly what happens at the beginning of your turn. It always causes a lot of amusement. I ask pupils to ski in a way which they know is ridiculous and is not how they would choose to ski at all. But when there is laughter the learning is not far behind. They discover for themselves what works efficiently for them, as you will. If I were to tell you the 'right' way of initiating a turn (even if there were one), you might create tension for yourself by striving to do it 'right'. You might start judging each turn and comparing it with your conception of what is 'right', and suddenly your self-image starts to get in on the act!

Make a game of experimenting with the range of possibilities; your awareness and feeling will be your teacher.

If you aren't sure which part of your body initiates the turn, ask a friend to tell you what they see.

WHICH PART OF YOUR BODY LEADS INTO THE TURN?

1 While you are skiing, notice which is the very first part of your body to lead into the turn. The choice ranges from the feet, knees, hips, through to the trunk, shoulders, arms and finally the head.

Compare the left and right turns and notice if there if a difference, and why? Remember there is no 'right' answer to this question; the value is in discovering it for yourself.

2 Now that you are focussing your awareness on the beginning of the turn, let's experiment by choosing to lead into the turn with various parts of the body. Some you will find awkward, some will be new, some may remind you of how you normally ski but all will result in an experience which will help you to learn what is effective, what is appropriate, and what works.

Start with your feet, twisting your outside one in the direction of your new turn. Then initiate the turn by pushing your outside knee over towards the inside one. Try the hips next, swinging them into your new direction, then your trunk and shoulders, and finally your head!

ANKLES – YOU CAN'T SKI WITHOUT THEM!

Look around at the stiff, awkward skiers on the mountain. Then look at their ankles. For some reason the ankle joint is often the first one to seize up through anxiety or trying too hard. Yet it is perhaps the most important connection between our 'control centre' and our skis.

Check them out for yourself. Standing on your skis, rock backwards until the back of your leg touches the back of the boot. Now move your knees from side to side and notice the effect, if any, on the angle of the skis. Bend your ankles forward until the tongue of your boot is pressing against your shin bone and move your knees sideways again. See the skis responding positively this time?

Though ski boots may feel as if your feet are encased in concrete they are designed to give you a lot of forward flexing whilst inhibiting sideways movement. Thus any sideways movement of the knees is transmitted directly to the ski edge.

When you are aware of the crucial part your ankles play in the skiing, whenever you feel stiff and uncoordinated just check down with the ankles and see what they are doing – you may find the missing link!

SKI FROM THE ANKLES

1 Ski whilst being totally aware of your ankles, particularly the ankle of the outside ski.
2 Follow its movement, or lack of it, throughout each turn. See if you can 'ski from the ankles'.
3 Stay with your ankles for two or three long runs noticing all the movements they make spontaneously, without any 'instructions' from you.
4 Stiffen up the ankles deliberately and ski with no movement or looseness anywhere. Does that remind you of how you feel sometimes? Then 'let go' of controlling the ankles. Feel the difference?

THE GEAR BOX

To give yourself more feedback about what your ankles are doing – and to help provide increased focus for your interest – imagine your lower leg is a gear lever and your ankle the gear box.

1 Rock your leg backwards until it touches the back of the boot – call that 'gear' neutral. Then rock forwards to the tongue of the boot, (that's first gear), squeeze the tongue a little bit (that's second gear), and squeeze it as hard as you can to find third gear.

2 Each time you turn call out loud the 'gear' you are in on the outside foot. It doesn't matter what gear you find yourself in, just call it out anyway.

3 Notice the difference between your left and right turns. Are the 'gears' different? Is the turn different?

4 Now choose the gear you want to ski in – from neutral to third gear, try them all in turn and see the different results.

5 Keep calling out! Not only will it help you be accurate in your awareness, it lessens the opportunity for distracting influences to creep in, and it helps with your breathing.

CRASHED YOUR GEARS AGAIN JOE?

HOW ARE YOUR KNEES?

Every skier knows the knees must be bent, mustn't they? Let's not make a rule about bending the knees – that's how the 'British lavatorial position' was created! Instead just focus on your knees and let them do the job of absorbing all the bumps, pressures and stresses of skiing.

THE 'SHOCK ABSORBERS'

1 Ski with awareness of your knees – notice what each is doing, particularly the one to the outside of each turn.

2 Is there any tension? If so how much on a scale of 1 to 10, and does it vary or remain constant?

3 Imagine your knees are the suspension of a motor car. Springs don't tense up just before a bump in the road – the wheels ride over it and the springs compress to absorb the impact. Let your knees be your 'springs' and notice the constant flexing as automatically they absorb every bump you ski over; notice too the pressure on them to the outside of every turn.

4 See if you 'feel' the terrain you are skiing over with your knees. They will tell you if only you will 'listen' to them!

THE KNEE CHASE GAME

At the beginning of each turn the 'outside' knee starts making 'advances' to the inside knee. The inside knee is coy and keeps moving away just out of reach. Just as it is about to catch up the 'inside' knee becomes the 'outside' and the game starts all over again!

KNEEL IN YOUR BOOTS!

When the whole business of knees just seems to confusing and you keep getting side-tracked into wondering what to do with them, and how bent 'should' they be, just kneel into your boots and let the tongue of the boot take the weight. Keep 'kneeling' as you ski the slope – it may feel as if your knees have never been so bent, but it can give you a clue as to how the knees will feel when you let them work to their maximum potential.

YOUR WEIGHT – WHERE IS IT?

Let's start by finding out how much weight you have on each foot as you ski. Stand with your eyes closed (on a quiet part of the slope!). Put 50 per cent of your weight on each foot. Now place 70 per cent of your weight on your uphill foot, now 70 per cent on the lower. Now 100 per cent on the lower, then 100 per cent on the top. Finally 60 per cent on the lower. Get used to what the different proportions of weight feel like. Open your eyes!

You've made your own scale of weight distribution, unique to you. It might not have been accurate, but when you have 70 per cent of weight according to your scale on one foot *you know what that feels like.* So armed with our new weight scale let's go and see what's happening!

These exercises can be done on any slope of your choice. My advice is that doing them on a simple slope first will be far more valuable than experimenting on a difficult mogul field. Why? Because feedback is what you're after, and you won't have much if other things start to interfere, like the steepness of the slope. I encourage pupils to try these exercises out on all slopes but we always start on a gentle slope first. There is much more learning here!

Now, let's ski noticing how much weight there is on the outside ski. We've only one thing to think about which I hope you'll find easy to manage! Focus on that ski and call out, as we do in our groups, the percentage weight on it. Notice the difference between the two turns. Remember, you're only *noticing what's happening,* you are not making it happen, at the moment. What are you calling out: 70, 60, 80 or maybe 70 one side, 80 the other?

Here's a little secret – it doesn't matter how much weight you have on which ski. It only matters that you know how much weight there is!

So if it doesn't matter how much weight there is, you'll find it a whole lot easier to be honest about reporting it. Like all the exercises in this book there is no 'right' or 'wrong'. You cannot fail or succeed in the doing, only in the reporting.

Most skiers at every standard have one turn which they prefer to the other. We don't have perfectly symmetrical bodies. At first in this exercise most skiers report a weight difference on their turns, calling a markedly higher number on one turn than the other. Ask yourself which is your favourite turn. Which turn has the most weight on the outside ski? Do you notice a connection? Is it the same side as your favoured turn, or the other? Don't let me spoil your experiment by telling you what I found. Find out for yourself!

Keep skiing for several hundred metres still staying with the exercise. Are you calling out the same numbers as you were at the beginning? If not, what's changed? Are you making the changes or merely reporting them? If you are not deliberately making the weights different, perhaps the body is picking up some feedback and putting in corrections of its own?

Now we are used to noticing how much weight there is on our outside ski, let's take it one stage further.
1 Use the whole of your scale, from 0 to 100 per cent if you like, to see how it feels to ski with varying weights. You'll find it easier at first playing about with the range between 50 per cent and 100 per cent, but later you can experiment all the way down to zero and see what happens!
2 What are your turns like at 80 per cent, 90 per cent and 100 per cent of your weight on the outside ski? Check them out several times. Do you notice the difference?
3 Look back and see if you can compare the lines in the snow left by the outside ski. Do you prefer one weight to another?
4 Remember the outside ski which used to have the lower weight of the two you called? What does that turn feel like now at 80 per cent, 90 per cent and 100 per cent?

Maybe you haven't been able to achieve every number – that doesn't matter. Come back to it later and have another go. There is learning going on at whatever level you want to take it. You are increasing your awareness of exactly what's happening, and feeding into your body new data for it to use.

Beware the trap! At this stage of the exercise pupils often see differences to their skiing happening very quickly. They try something slightly out of their accustomed range, discover something new and like it!

Now comes the inevitable question: "How much weight *should* there be on the outside ski?" After a couple of days on the course no one asks the question, but it's really popular at the beginning! My answer is always "I don't know", which is hardly the 'tip of the week' they thought they were going to get!

Knowing the dilemma I will ski for a few turns calling out the weight on *my* skis. Inevitably it won't be constant and can vary between 70 per cent and 100 per cent.

"Well, you heard what I was doing then, and that felt comfortable to me". I think they get the point. There are so many variables such as the terrain, the speed and the radius of the turn that to give a definitive answer is clearly nonsense. The weight is a constantly varying factor and you will never establish an optimum figure. What you *will* discover is the kind of weight at which *you feel happiest.* You'll notice the kind of turns you are producing and your body will pick up the correlation itself. It doesn't need you to spell it out. Remember the trust element!

Let's recap on this exercise and see what we got out of it.

- We learned to recognise and assess one of the fundamental basics of skiing – the weighted ski.
- We discovered the effect on our turns and on our skiing of applying the complete range of weight, and found out what works and what doesn't work in a wide variety of circumstances.
- We let the body get on with the learning and kept the 'mind' or ego distracted from trying to help.
- We learned that trying to copy some arbitrary 'norm' is limiting to our learning and is rarely effective.
- We established that varying the weight on each ski is

indeed one of the 'parts' of the whole flowing movement. How it varies for *you* only *you* can tell.

In conclusion

We've taken the risk of falling into the trap I mentioned earlier of examining one part of the whole moving body of parts. The trap closes when you try and make that part perform in a pre-established way. The trap disappears when the focus is applied merely for letting the body explore and learn.

LOOKING AT YOUR EDGES

What are your edges doing as you ski? There is an easy way to find out – look at them!

1 Stand with your skis flat on the snow. On a slope I often find that means that the bottom ski is left to support my weight, while I open up the top ski to lay it flat on the snow just above me.

2 With your top ski flat call that position '0' for no edge. Then put the ski on its inside edge and find the maximum angle you can reach. Call that a '3'. Now on your scale find where a '2' and a '1' would be. Easy so far?

3 Start skiing on a straightforward slope, and notice or

THE WEIGHT ON THE
OUTSIDE SKI

call out the degree of edging on the outside ski during the turn, using your scale so you won't have too much difficulty assessing it. If it's not easy or you don't think your answer is very accurate, slow down, or find safer terrain until you can pinpoint your degree of edge with certainty.

4 Ask yourself these questions:

- What number am I calling?
- Is my right turn different from my left?
- On which number am I happiest?
- If the numbers are changing – why? Is the slope changing in steepness or contours?
- Begin to notice your speed round the turn. Is it different when you call different numbers?
- Look at the radius of the turn. Does this vary according to the numbers?

5 Up to now you have just been aware of your edging. Now aim to edge a ski at one of the numbers on your scale. Test the whole range; do it for the sake of experiencing the whole range, *not* because one number is better than another. Look at the differences and the results. Some of these edge positions you may never have experienced before. How do different degrees of edge affect your skiing?

6 Now you have the ability to focus on your edging, try some steeper and more difficult slopes. The interferences and distractions will increase but see if you can still stay focussed. *The inside edge of the outside ski* is the point where most of the forces acting on your body are concentrated. The feedback from this exercise is vital to fluid skiing. Don't judge how much edge there ought to be, just see how much edge there is!

TOWARDS MORE FLUID SKIING

I often ask pupils the question "Imagine yourself skiing as you would really like – how would you look?" After a short think they usually reply it would look "really smooth", "fluent", "fluid", "graceful", "elegant", "flowing". They are visualising in their mind skiers they have admired. They don't pick up on one aspect of their skiing like the position of their shoulders, the timing of their pole plant or the movement of their hips. The impression the skier leaves is a quality which includes all these but is something else as well.

What is conveyed to someone watching a good skier, or indeed any accomplished athlete, is an appearance of gracefulness. When everything is working efficiently like a well-oiled machine there appears to be no wasted effort, no forced movements, a flowing rhythm of power. I call it "fluid skiing".

The beauty comes from the whole movement and the

THE BUTTON EXERCISE

This game takes the 'trying' out of turning and lets the ski make its own line from start to finish.

1 Pretend there is a push-button on the outside of each of your knees: let's call them button A and button B.

2 Keep a finger on each button as you ski and each time you want to change direction just press one of the buttons! Start off in a snow-plough if you like until you get the hang of it, but then do whatever feels comfortable, just keep pressing those buttons.

3 Are you *trying* to turn or are you trusting your buttons? You can tell the difference by checking for tension in your legs, or feeling your hips wanting to help you turn!

4 Experiment with pressing the buttons like a child would with a new toy. What happens when you press them harder? With different pressures on each? At longer and shorter intervals?

5 Notice the arc each outside ski is making. Is it uniform and smooth? Are you letting the ski find its own line?

6 Although your position is exaggerated you may experience something of the dynamic balance of a ski racer! It can be tiring, though, so after each turn stand up, let the blood flow back into the thighs, then just before the next turn press the button on the outside of the uphill knee and ride round the turn on that ski.

way it is in harmony with the terrain. No wonder we stop and watch when around us all over the mountain we see examples of jerkiness, forced turns, flailing arms and crashed bodies and skis.

Beware!

We are about to walk into a trap – a trap that waits for every skier who starts to think about improving their skiing. It goes like this: you see a skier you admire flying effortlessly down a run which has just caused you almighty problems. He is making beautiful linked S-turns, one flowing into the next. Just the chance for a useful lesson! You watch carefully what he's doing. "Ah, I see, he's planting his pole just below his foot, and he's bending his lower leg more than his upper." You might notice also that he moves his weight over to his top ski very early in the turn, and seems to lift the lower ski off the ground for an instant. He was skiing past us for only ten seconds and we've got four valuable tips! Now we've got something to practise; pole plant, knees, early weight transfer and lifting one ski. But which one first?

After a few minutes another skier comes past looking as elegant as the first. You watch what he's doing: he's planting his pole in quite a different place and he's not lifting his ski at all. You can't even see him transferring his weight; maybe he isn't, and that's the answer? "This is nothing like I was going to practise – which one do I choose? Help, what *is* the right way to do it?"

Well, here we are in the trap! What is it? Simply, **the movement of skiing is more than the sum of its parts.** Otherwise, we would ski like clockwork soldiers. Clockwork soldiers march mechanically, everything working to precision. But where are the qualities we were looking for earlier – smoothness and fluency? Do

you really want to ski like clockwork? If you break down skiing into its constituent parts you are left only with a heap of parts. Put them together and the cracks will show!

If skiing was simply about perfecting each movement from your big toe up to your head, wouldn't it be straightforward? On a week's course we could spend a day getting each section right and by Friday afternoon you'd be an elegant skier!

This is the dilemma

Analyse a good skier and you learn a lot about what he's doing. Attempt to re-create what he's doing as precisely as you can, and frustratingly you don't end up with a good skier. It just doesn't work that way. And there's more. You will never be that skier, ever. In trying to be you will slow down your learning, and create disappointment always. But what you can learn and achieve is far more valuable and permanent. You can ski expressing the same *qualities* in your skiing as he does in his. Isn't that what you want from your skiing? – grace, fluency and harmony.

We'll get there by another route. We won't analyse someone else and copy them. We'll look at *ourselves* and see how efficiently each part of us is working and make adjustments if they are needed. Then we can ski trusting each part of our body to do its job. Once we are confident that the parts of our body know how to work, we can let the whole body get on with the skiing, and the efficiency of movement will produce the gracefulness in you to match the skier you've admired.

In this part of the course we're going to look closely at each bit of the 'fluid' movement of our body and skis. But we are not going to fall into the trap! By examining every movement, we let our body do the learning. We will let it *feel* the actions and *feel* the results of those actions. We will give our bodies a blank canvas on which to experiment. There are no results known in advance, there is no forcing it to copy some vision of what you think is the 'right' way to do it. There is just going to be learning – naturally, and allowing the body to do what it wants to do most: ski well.

And now for some action

Ski a slope that's comfortably within your standard for a few hundred metres. Don't try to ski in any particular way. In fact don't *try* to ski! Notice any tension or tightness in your body. It may be more pronounced on one turn than the other. Notice whether your body tenses at any particular part of the turn, or if there's a feeling of tension all the time. If you notice and locate any tension at all, you've taken a major step towards more fluid skiing.

I'd like you now to continue skiing in the same way but become more and more interested in the part of your body that is producing 'stress'. It may be in an arm, in your hands as they grip the poles, or in the toes as they are scrunched up in the boots refusing to let go of their grip on the sole.

Here is another trap coming up: **Don't try to relax!** We're aiming for fluid skiing, and relaxing is not going to achieve that for us.

"But whenever I see a good skier he always looks so relaxed", you cry. "Now you are telling me I mustn't relax!" You're right. Good skiers are relaxed, but they don't get that way by deliberately relaxing. They are relaxed because their bodies are working efficiently

and they trust their body and skis to get on with the job. (Note that word 'trusting' again. You see what a vital part of this learning method it is.)

"So if relaxing is not the game we're playing, what *are* we playing?" Ah, now we're going to discover something extraordinary about the ability of our bodies to learn. The tension you experience in your body is telling you something about your skiing. By wishing it wasn't there you're wishing away one of the most valuable pieces of information about your skiing you could possibly have. Your body is telling you something and here you are ignoring it. No instructor, no film, no video will give you feedback like it. The tension you feel is the key to what you are looking for; and where's your mind? Wishing your skis were closer together, or thinking about the awful turn three turns ago!

Let's call this game the 'tension game'. When you've located a tension stay with it. See if you can report on it to yourself with the detachment of an inspector reading your electricity meter. He's not interested in the results, or thinking about how large your bill is going to be this quarter. He's interested in getting the reading right and recording it accurately. If you can be as detached as that during all the games, drills and experiments we're going to do, 'miracles' will happen. Mind you, it *will* be a miracle if you can stay that detached from such a serious matter as your own skiing! That's the model to aim for, though.

THE TENSION GAME

1 Stay with the tension, notice when it gets less and when it increases. Sometimes a pupil will say "But I'm tense everywhere". Don't complain about so much feedback, but focus in on one place only, usually the most obvious because you feel most tension there.

2 See if you can make a scale for your tension, giving it 10 for maximum and a zero for how you imagine it would feel when relaxed.

3 How tense is it now? Where in the turn is it at its highest? And its lowest? Compare left and right turns.

4 Call out the number on your scale each time it reaches the highest tension on the turn. Don't be afraid of calling it out loud – no one's going to mind, and it might help your accuracy.

Remember, it's the accuracy which is important – not your opinion about it. Why do I emphasise this? Because if the body is going to learn it needs *facts*, not opinions or judgements. The facts will enable your body to respond and self-correct. Amazing, but it's true; doing it for yourself will prove it. Your body is no fool. It does not want to be tense and awkward any more than you do! Let it know exactly what's happening. Give it the details of where, when, how often, how much, and let it sort out the problem for itself.

An observer might see something in your skiing which is blocking your freedom of movement. Telling you is of limited help. Because we do not know the micro-movements of each muscle and their relationship with each other an outsider's description of 'what is wrong' is most likely to be inaccurate. Even if we try to analyse it ourselves we don't have the knowledge to place every moving bone and muscle in its optimum position. Heavens, I don't know the names of most of what's inside me! I know I cannot work out the corrections myself – but I know my body can.

Here's the proof! Stay with this exercise for a couple of runs, concentrating on the accuracy of your reporting. See if a pattern is building up. Is the tension the same or are the numbers changing? If they are changing, are they getting higher or lower? Keep at it a little longer and begin to notice what changes are taking place.

Why do I know that changes are happening? Because when you become closely aware of what your body is doing while you are skiing, changes will always happen. This is how the body learns. The awareness itself allows change to happen.

HOW THE 'TENSION GAME' CAN WORK

On one of my recent courses, a pupil expressed dissatisfaction with her turns to the left. She said her right turns were OK but the left ones felt laboured and jerky. Indeed when I watched her I could see a big difference: her right turns were an effective 'carve' and the left were skidded, with her bottom ski dragging along interfering with her momentum. It was also obvious that our exercise of looking for spots of tension was a long way from what she wanted to do. She felt she wasn't skiing as well as she was last year and until she was she couldn't concentrate on any new lessons.

"Would you do an experiment for me for fifteen minutes" I asked her, "then we'll come back to your left turns. Tell me how tense the leg on the outside of each turn is out of ten, and call it out loud as you go round." "Seven", "two", "seven", "two", "seven", "two", she called. "Good; just keep noticing the tension and carry on skiing."

We skied the slope and there was little change. At the bottom I asked her not to make corrections nor try to make the seven and the two more equal. The game was to be accurate, just calling the score without changing it herself. I let her go up the lift for a run on her own continuing the drill. I stayed at the bottom and next time she arrived there was little change. Was she still playing the game or had she changed the rules? She wanted to stick with it for the sake of the experiment and I guessed her patience was good for one more run. She passed me halfway down the next run. I'd heard her long before, calling "seven", "two", "seven", "two", "six", "two", "six", "two", "five", "two", "four", "two", "three", "two", "three", "two", "two", "two". When I caught up with her she was grinning from ear to ear. "I've never skied like that before. Phew!" I could see the change in her skiing, her turns were more uniform and she looked far smoother.

What had happened? It was not magic. Her body already knew what a 'good' turn felt like – she was doing one every other turn. Now it was recognizing the difference between each turn. The tension wasn't *making* the difference, it was only the symptom. But the body worked out the difference and quietly made the corrections. The big lesson had been learned, and her skiing improved dramatically during the week.

What caused that tension?
There are many explanations but only one root cause: a lack of trust that the body or the skis won't do what's appropriate to keep you skiing smoothly and efficiently at all times. It's that simple!

COMMITMENT

When you have a '10 out of 10' commitment to an exercise, that's when amazing things happen. When your commitment is less than 10 you're wide open to other influences that you don't want. Here are some examples:

- "I'll do this exercise for a few seconds to see if I think it's worth doing before I commit myself to doing it properly."
- "I wonder what he's getting at?" – "What are we supposed to be discovering by doing that?"
- "This skiing is too easy – I'd rather be doing a black run."
- "I wonder what I *should* be doing with my ankles."
- "I think I'm the worst skier in the group – but I don't want to go to a lower one."
- "I rather fancy the girl in the pink anorak".

Can you imagine the kind of feedback your body is receiving when it has all this static on the line?

So how can we make sure our commitment level is 10 out of 10? It's easy – the answer is "You can choose!" Then it's up to you. You can choose to do an exercise or drill, or not. If you choose to do it you might as well use the time effectively and do it with a high commitment – why choose to do it with a low commitment? If after a few minutes you stop to reflect on what you have just done, ask yourself the question "How *committed* was I to looking at the effect of (say) moving the position of my ankles?" If the answer is 6 out of 10 then don't be discouraged if you derived little benefit. If something else about your skiing, like the position of your hands, seems more interesting then explore that and come back to the original exercise later.

Please don't kid yourself!
The exercises and games in this book have *all* produced the most amazing breakthroughs and learning experiences in people's skiing. For me they are all 'gold-plated' as I've seen them working over many years. But not all of them work for everybody. If one doesn't work for you, look at another one. You can afford to be extravagant – just one exercise in this book could revolutionize your skiing. Please don't discard or reject any of them without trying it first with a very high commitment level. Fifty metres of skiing with all your attention on the focus in question can achieve the breakthrough you want. A week spent doing everything in this book with half of your attention is a complete waste of time and money!

Generally your commitment level is high when your interest is high. You don't have to *try* to focus your attention. Go where your interest is high, then it is easy. If you are concerned that your bottom is sticking out while you are skiing, where will your interest be during an exercise to do with pole-planting? I sometimes ask my pupils to choose which of the exercises they have done in the past day or so gave them the *least* value. When they call them out there is usually much amusement because often someone's least favourite has been another's breakthrough! Then I ask them all if they would like to ski, by way of an experiment, focussing on their least favourite exercise for just two minutes with a 100 per cent commitment level. For two minutes they figure out they can choose to do that, if only to please me! There is always at least one member of the group who, after a short run, has made some amazing discovery they can't wait to share with the others.

The value of this book lies totally in the commitment you put into each experiment.

How much do you want to become a fluid skier?

SUMMING UP THE SECOND DAY'S SKIING

It's been a busy day of discovery – discovering our skis and how they work, finding out just how much our body does even without us telling it, and exploring the effects of raising our awareness on our skiing. Tomorrow we'll take it a step further, learn to increase our trust in our body as we ski, and try some games that will help our technique and give us confidence in poor visibility.

Third Day

By today you will have thoroughly re-discovered your ski legs as well as having experienced how it feels to begin trusting your skis and your body.

Now we are going to look at some games which require vivid use of the imagination and which will help you to discover techniques which can work for you.

We look at fear, lack of trust and self-doubt, and we finish the day with some exercises to do next time you find yourself skiing in poor visibility.

Whenever we are taught something unfamiliar, in order to succeed we are told to 'try'. If success doesn't come at first our teacher, parents and friends suggest we 'try harder'.

I'd like you to 'try' a few things now – really 'try'. Try

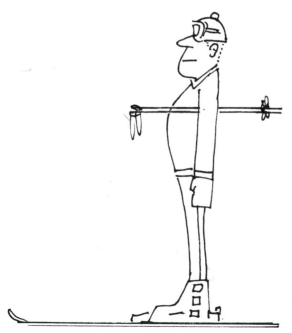

holding your ski poles, try holding this book, try and walk in a straight line without moving your head, try and smile. Try and breathe deeply. In all these 'tries' you will be involving muscles and energy you don't need – surplus to requirements. When you tried to hold this book did your grip on it tighten even though you were holding it perfectly adequately before? Let's see what it is like to ski without the 'trying' effect. But can you try *not* to try? Here are one or two games I play with groups of skiers when they see for themselves that they don't have to try!

SKI AS STIFFLY AS YOU CAN

Tighten up every muscle in your body, starting with your toes through to your face. All tightened up? OK, now ski! I always love watching the faces of the other skiers when our group staggers down looking like wooden soldiers or robots. And as for what they think of the teacher! Interesting things come out of this exercise:

1 It is possible to ski and yet be ridiculously stiff.

2 It is not very nice to do it for long – there must be an easier way to ski!

3 Some skiers don't like to play this game with much commitment. Their self-image is at risk!

4 There is learning in looking at the whole spectrum of body tension – if only to see the effect of the high end of the scale!

AUDITION FOR THE BALLET

In the ballet 'Coppelia' the dolls in the toyshop come to life at night when the owner closes up and goes home. Slowly the dolls ease their stiff joints and gradually come to life.

Pretend you're auditioning for a part in a new 'alpine' production of the ballet. Start your run as stiff as one of those dolls or toys. Act the part as you ski. Then starting with your toes gradually loosen up the muscles, slowly moving up through the legs, buttocks, chest, arms and hands, neck and finally face.

Finish the run as loose as a puppet on strings. Many is the time when the group, having got so involved with the game, have let their bodies carry on relaxing through the puppet stage and beyond to finally end up in a slow sprawl on the ground where they tell me they've become a jelly or even an amoeba!

After the first trial audition I always ask them "How much of you was a stiff, rigid toy at the beginning if, on a scale of 1 to 10, 10 is as stiff as you could possibly imagine?" or "How floppy were you at the end if 0 was as floppy as you could imagine?" The replies intrigue me, everybody keeps something in hand! When we try it again many report 10's and 0's and the value of the lesson is appreciated, and parts are awarded in the new production! The learning?

1 Firstly it always causes amusement, and where there's enjoyment learning is never far away.

2 When the intention is to be tense, as at the beginning of the game, relaxation seems to interfere!

3 Your body has experienced yet another complete range of tension.

4 The floppy bit at the end is a new sensation and often leads to requests to explore it further.

THE 'TOTALLY FLOPPY' GAME

Many skiers achieve a breakthrough in their quests for more fluid skiing while playing this game.

1 Imagine something really floppy or limp. I use the image of a rag-doll, whilst others think of a wilting flower or sometimes even a blancmange!

2 Ski your next slope being that rag-doll (or blancmange!). Pick a slope you would generally find a little bit of a challenge.

3 With your head drooping over your skis, your arms hanging limply in front of you, your sticks merely resting in your hand, you certainly don't look like the text-book image of a skier!

4 How does it feel: how balanced are you, how relaxed are you, how floppy are you?

5 Keep going looking for more challenging terrain. What are you noticing about your skiing?

Here are some of the comments I've heard from a group doing this exercise:

- "Hey, I never used my poles once – I didn't need to!"
- "My legs seemed to absorb all the bumps."
- "I felt so much more relaxed."
- "I could go on doing that all day."
- "I felt I wasn't trying at all, almost resting, but I was skiing well!"

6 If, on a scale of 1 to 10, your floppiness was 10, how would it be to ski with a floppiness of 8?

TEN PLUS, PETER

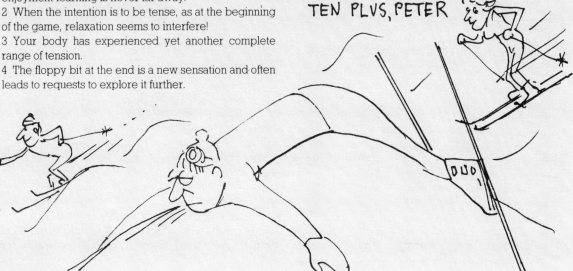

Conclusion

Some of the images we use in our games can sound silly but using them gives us an experience we would have missed otherwise. Maybe a totally floppy skier is not what we want to be, but by being one for a bit we have seen what it is like to ski on the other side of the 'stiffness' pendulum. On the way, our body will have picked up a point at which everything seems to be working in harmony – something it will find much harder to do with a theoretical approach to skiing.

RECOGNISING THE FORCES ACTING ON THE SKIER

Wherever we are, whatever we are doing, there are forces acting on us. Our body either responds appropriately or we lose our balance.

As we stand still on a pavement the main force is gravity acting through our body keeping our feet on the ground. If a strong wind blows we lean into it, our weight at this angle counteracting the force of the wind trying to blow us over.

As we saw from our experiment on page 15, when we stand on a roundabout there is a force on our body trying to pull us off. The body resists this by moving our centre of gravity away from the pull, towards the centre of the roundabout, to counteract its effect.

"That's easy", I can hear you say, "I don't slip on a pavement, and there's plenty of friction between my shoes and the roundabout to keep me balanced. Snow is very different!"

Yes, snow *is* different, and of course there is much less friction (which allows us to slide and enjoy the result). But we have one big advantage: we are wearing skis on snow. Let's discover what they do to keep us balanced – using an illustration which Ali Ross, the well-known British ski instructor, once showed me.

1 Stand on a slope sideways, comfortably on your skis.

2 Grip your lower pole as if it were a hammer and let somebody standing below you pull at the other end firmly down the hill. Resist the pull naturally, and don't allow yourself to be moved away from where you are standing.

3 As the pull becomes stronger notice the position you are having to allow the body to find in order to both resist the pull and keep balanced.

Here you are standing on a slippery surface of snow, on a smooth ski designed to minimize friction, and yet you haven't moved in spite of the force pulling you downhill! How come?

Look at your skis! The edges have angled themselves to create a solid platform against the pull. You don't feel as if you are about to slip off down the hill, do you?

The angle of our skis enables us to overcome the lack of friction. The greater the pull, the greater the angle of the skis.

You can prove it works for any skier, by pulling on your companion's downhill pole. From beginners to the very experienced they will all adopt very similar positions. They have to, otherwise they'd fall downhill!

One thing I notice when trying this exercise with pupils is that the beginners always, at first, look more natural resisting the downward pull of the ski stick than the intermediate skiers. That's because the only way they can stay upright is to find a balanced position

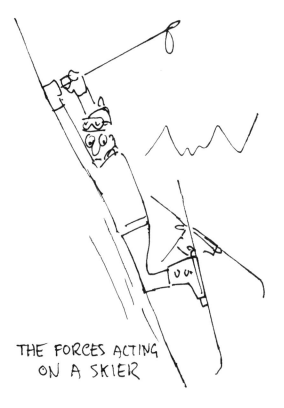

THE FORCES ACTING ON A SKIER

naturally. The others think they know a technique. That gets in the way of the naturalness, and one tug and they're over! But they soon learn. Next time I won't shift them however hard I pull!

Notice the shape your body makes when naturally resisting the pull of a force. Look where your hips are. Which hip is ahead of the other? Look at your shoulders, your legs and your knees. Indeed, look where you are looking. If you are concerned about technique you are producing it in abundance, perfectly! I know, because if you weren't you'd have been pulled downhill by your companion.

The body will respond appropriately to any force acting on it, if it is allowed to.

Beware! The converse is not true. In attempting to reproduce the body position by analysing it you are not allowing the body to respond naturally and imbalance occurs!

I can remember clearly when learning to ski that I had a mental checklist I would go over at the beginning of every traverse across a slope. Before I set off I'd make sure that:
- my top ski was ahead of the lower;
- my weight was mostly on the bottom ski;
- my top shoulder was advanced;
- my hips were in towards the mountain;
- I was looking vaguely downhill.

I believed that in obeying all those 'rules' I would learn to ski – I took a long time to learn, and no wonder!

As we can see, the effect on the body resisting any force pulling on it results in the kind of body position you have just achieved in the above exercise. It is more or less exaggerated according to the degree of the force. It's what you discover works for you in each instance. Each of our bodies is different as will be the forces on them. Rules are irrelevant!

"OK", you say, "I can see that when I'm standing still, but it's not the same when I'm moving!" Isn't it?

Imagine you are twirling a weight around your head on a piece of string. If the string broke the momentum of the weight would cause it to fly off at right angles to the circle it was making. Wherever the weight is there is a constant pull away from the centre of the circle.

As we turn on skis we are like that weight being pulled outwards from the centre of the arc of our turn. Just as we resisted the pull straight down the hill when somebody

SKIING BY THE RULES

tugged on our ski pole, so we naturally resist the pull throughout the turn.

The ski-pole trick is a way of illustrating the forces of your body at one point of the turn. During an actual turn, you will experience an outwards pull made up of a combination of your momentum pulling in one direction and gravity pulling downhill. The direction of the resulting combined force can only be felt in practice – on the move. The forces vary during the turn, and the body can learn to produce an unlimited range of responses.

In one simple experiment we explored the body's ability to respond to forces acting upon it. We can now take our learning in one of two directions:
- Reproduce our analysis of the 'appropriate' body position and try to make the body fit all the forces we are going to meet in future, OR
- Reproduce a range of different forces and let the body find the appropriate response to each.

By now I think you'll guess the route we'll follow!

PAINTING YOUR WAY DOWNHILL

The 'paint brush' is one of my favourite exercises. It encourages rhythm, grace and balance, and most importantly it enables us to create an exaggerated pull, or force, to allow the body to find its own response. This response awakens our awareness and reminds us we do not have to 'make' anything happen in order to remain perfectly balanced on skis as we turn.

1 Imagine that you are holding in each hand not your ski pole, but large paint brushes.

2 You have just dipped them in a tin of black Indian ink and you are standing on your skis at the top of a huge sheet of white parchment paper.

3 On each turn describe beautiful arcs in the snow with your 'outside' paint brush. Vary the imaginary brush-stroke: firm strokes and light ones; large arcs and narrow ones; broken lines and flowing lines.

4 Vary the colours. Imagine and choose your own. Really 'see' the strokes you are making; what does the pattern look like in the snow behind you?

5 Notice when in the turn you start the stroke – right at the beginning or part of the way through? See how early in the turn you can start the stroke. Then see if you can start it later!

6 How far from you can you make the stroke? What differences do you feel in your body shape when the stroke is as far from you as you can reach, compared with a stroke right by your side?

7 Remember the earlier exercise of someone pulling your ski pole down the hill. Do you recognise the similarities with the 'paint brush'?

8 Notice how straight your arm is. If it is bent, how would it react to imagining a thicker brush-stroke, applied with more pressure?

9 Where are you beginning your imaginary brush-stroke – immediately to your side, behind your boots or in front of them? It makes a difference. Notice the difference and find out which you prefer.

How did you feel about your skiing after you tried this exercise? Were you aware of one turn flowing into another – and if so, can you see why? *Did you turn the skis or did the skis turn you?* Did you enjoy it?

You can get out your paint brush anywhere – moguls, piste, powder. It will always smooth your path!

THE MYTH OF 'CHANGING YOUR WEIGHT'

I can remember being taught that in order to turn I must transfer my weight from one ski to another and the weighted ski would turn me round. It was always unclear as to how much weight you transfer and when you transfer it.

The answer was given to me in a totally unexpected way. For that I am again indebted to Ali Ross. Try his suggestion and see what you discover.

1 Have a companion pull at your downhill ski stick whilst you resist this force.

2 On which ski is most of your weight? The lower or upper one?

3 Ask your companion to let go of the stick. Where is your weight now? On the upper one?

You see what I mean? As a result of a change in the force acting on you, your weight transferred from one foot to the other. You didn't transfer it, did you? It just transferred!

The myth is you must transfer your weight in order to turn. The reality is that between one turn and another the forces acting on you change, and as a consequence your weight transfers. The amount of weight and the timing of the transfer cannot be pre-determined. Trust your body to sort it out!

THE LASER BEAM IN YOUR FINGER-TIPS

Another exercise in imagery produces results from unexpected quarters, whilst also increasing your awareness of the 'pull' upon you from the outside of your turns.

1 Imagine your forefinger of each hand is a laser gun firing a steady stream of intensely bright particles of light. As the beam hits the snow it 'sizzles' as it melts it, leaving a blackened scorch mark in its wake.

2 Let the forefinger of the outside hand fire the beam as you go round the turn. Keep the beam aimed at the snow from the beginning of the turn to the end.

3 What colour is your beam? The more you can 'see' it, the more powerful and helpful the image will be for you.

4 At the beginning of the next turn let the other 'gun' take over! Keep your aim straight and follow the trail of 'smoke' you are making. You can make sound effects for this one, imitating the hissing noise the burnt snow is making!

Do you enjoy visualising the effects you are making? When it's enjoyable, concentration is easiest. With concentration comes absorption, and then other distractions (like thoughts of 'how should I turn?') have difficulty in finding their expression. Fortunately!

What effect does this exercise have on your skiing? We've been discussing forces acting on you in a turn and duplicating or exaggerating them to see how we respond. One of the things I notice with pupils playing the Laser Game is how neat their arms are, and how balanced they look. But that's purely by the way!

SO WHAT 'BLOCKS' THE BALANCED POSITION?

By now you have a feel of how the body behaves when balanced throughout a turn. We've also seen from these exercises that the body will balance itself, naturally, given the chance. But sometimes the body is blocked from being allowed to express its natural movement. Why?

We've looked at reasons for this throughout the book, but here are three of the most common:
1 Fear or anxiety.
2 Self-doubt and lack of trust.
3 Trying to look good!

FEAR

Fear is never far away from our thoughts when we are skiing: fear of injury, fear of falling, fear of failing (in our own eyes or in those of others), fear of looking stupid. And fear can really get in the way of our skiing.

However real your fear may be, its *cause* may be real or imaginary. A response to a true danger, such as a slope avalanching above you, can be dramatic. The body reacts with a rush of adrenalin which heightens alertness, calms the thought processes and increases strength and agility. Many is the skier who has skied for his life at a level way above his usual limits to avoid being caught by an avalanche.

Most causes of fear, however, are largely imaginary. The reaction of a skier traversing a slope which he perceives as steeper than it actually is will be quite different. The mind becomes clogged with 'what if' instead of 'what is'; the body tenses, movement becomes restricted, everything becomes more difficult to do, and efficiency is greatly reduced.

Handling the interference of fear

As we've seen already most fear is caused by our 'little voice' or ego telling us to be afraid. It makes judgements like

- "This slope is too steep".
- "This is the kind of slope I broke my leg on".
- "This snow is horrible!"

These provide the ammunition for fear; and we are all too ready to listen.

The exercises, drills and games throughout this book have one thing in common. They create the opportunity to focus the ego so completely on one specific event that there is no room for fear to distract you. The degree to which we can absorb and interest the ego with other matters is the degree to which we will conquer fear in our skiing. Start on easy slopes first: practise totally absorbing the ego mind with an exercise in a relaxed mode before attempting to block out totally the distractions of fear on the steeper stuff!

Mis-perceptions

Another way of coping with an 'imagined' fear is to become clear about exactly what is frightening you. Stop and look carefully at the next slope that scares you. How steep is it really? How long is it? How big are the moguls and where are they? Where is the soft snow and where are the icy bits? When you replace judgements and perceptions with the truth, you have come a long way towards reducing the effect of fear.

Choice

When you perceive a situation accurately and are still afraid (or choose to be afraid), you have a further choice to make. To ski it, or find an alternative route. Weighing up the facts and choosing your course of action will help you master the handicap of fear.

SELF-DOUBT AND LACK OF TRUST

When you don't totally trust yourself or your skis, or you doubt your ability to perform as well as you would like, the ego is only too willing to come in and lend a hand. The guise it uses is 'trying' and the degree of trying is directly proportional to the lack of trust or the amount of self-doubt you are demonstrating.

'Trying' has clearly recognisable symptoms: tension, stiffness, tight muscles, irregular breathing, increased pulse rate. All these things interfere with and restrict free, flowing, effortless skiing. The exercises in this book are designed to neutralise the effect of 'trying' and to encourage trust in yourself and your skis.

Experiencing our skis working successfully in the way they were designed – even, or perhaps particularly, on a nursery slope – will quickly eliminate lack of trust in our skis as being the excuse for effort.

We can then let our skis do their job and our bodies can be left to discover and enjoy the optimum balanced position which the drills in the book are helping you to find.

TRYING TO LOOK GOOD!

This is almost universal. Skiers have a natural inclination to want to impress. There are exceptions, but the clothing designers, the sunglass manufacturers, the equipment shops and the sellers of suntan cream are happy that they are rare.

Our egos have much to say about 'looking good' and their advice and instruction produce many of the same tensions in the body that imagined fear does. Although the exercises in this chapter are not obviously to do with looking good, they will all help you achieve that aim. When you are balanced on your skis, trusting them to turn you and enjoying the experience, you'll be looking good too. When you are concerned with how you look and trying to engineer your body to produce what you think are the 'looking good' movements, you'll be joining all the other duffers on the slopes!

THE MYTH OF 'SKIING PARALLEL'

When I ask pupils what they'd really like to achieve in the week, the most frequent wish is to ski with parallel skis. Indeed, the term 'parallel skier' denotes in many peoples' minds an accomplished skier, a standard to aspire to!

I always ask them *why* they wish to ski with their skis always parallel and they usually say it is because they see the experts doing it and it looks good.

Yes, it's true, experienced, confident skiers frequently have their skis parallel and quite close together. They also quite frequently have their skis at an angle to each other and far from together. The three points to note here are:

1 The 'good' skier is one who responds to changing terrain and conditions with every technique at his disposal. To limit himself to enforced parallel skiing is to deny many manoeuvres which a skier needs to smooth out his path as he descends the unevenness of a mogul slope.

2 Skis come together and are parallel purely as a result of the forces acting on them in a turn. With one ski bearing most of the weight during a turn, the other is allowed to drift round with it. It inevitably ends up close to and parallel to the outside ski. So efficient skiing produces the 'parallel' look. The parallel look does not, however, produce efficient skiing. Which would you rather have?

3 When we spend time on a nursery slope, and we're pressing button A's and B's (see Day 2), I'm often asked what this has to do with parallel skiing. The answer is, of course, everything! The response of the body to the forces exerted upon it whilst turning in a snow-plough or a 'parallel' are the same. The inside leg is merely a support to balance the body at a slow speed. At higher speeds the pull on the inside leg will produce a 'parallel' merely because it is more appropriate. The 'snow-plough' is a most maligned turn. It is rarely performed with grace and dignity even when it is appropriate. Its nursery-slope associations have given it the image of a discarded teddy bear. So it becomes unloved and unwanted, and performed only in dire emergencies by everybody except the expert skier. The expert? Yes, watch any slalom racer and you'll recognise the snow-plough as the basis of their technique.

THE FINAL WORD ON TRUSTING YOUR SKIS

Skiers who don't trust their skis to turn them find all sorts of ways to avoid having to trust them. Look around you on the mountain and you'll see what I mean – much twisting and rotating of bodies and shoulders to drive those skis round the corners. Isn't there an easier, more efficient way to get the skis to work for you? There is, and it takes one important step. **You will need to give up forever the notion that skis will turn only with a great deal of effort from you**. If you've been brought up to believe anything

worth having is only achieved by struggle, you will find it a difficult philosophy to give up! This next exercise which I call the 'Commitment Side-Step' lets the ski do all the work, and may prove to you its amazing capability when you totally commit yourself to it and trust it!

THE COMMITMENT SIDE-STEP

Our groups play this game whatever their skiing level. You can play it on any slope however flat or steep – even off-piste, particularly on crud or breakable crust. Like all our games there are no rules and you can play around with it and discover from it what you can.

1 When one turn is complete and you are approaching the next, lift up your uphill ski and firmly place it down on the snow a little further uphill from you, pointing in the direction you want to turn. As the ski strikes the snow say the word 'now' to coincide exactly with the action.

2 Are you on time? Ask a companion to check it out for you and tell you.

3 Play around with the sound of the word 'now' – make it louder or softer. Match it to the action of your ski: loud for an aggressive side-step, soft for a lighter one!

4 How much is the ski edged as it hits the ground? Make up a scale for edging, giving 0 to a flat ski and 5 to the maximum edge you can manage. Call out the numbers as that ski hits the snow testing the effects at the various numbers.

5 How much weight are you putting on that ski – 50 per cent, 80 per cent, 100 per cent?

6 Notice if you are beginning to introduce other things into the game. Check out hips and shoulders for signs of 'assistance'!

7 What are you experiencing from this exercise? Here are a few examples from people who have tried it:

- "The moment of being balanced on one ski had a calming influence and I tried to make it last longer and longer."
- "The ski just took me round. I didn't have to do anything, it was amazing."
- "Whenever I'm in difficulties I go back to the 'commitment side-step' and it gets me out of trouble, even on a plastic ski slope!"
- "I've always hated the off-piste till now."
- "I couldn't lift up one ski to save my life!"

There's a lot of learning in all those findings, and you'll probably discover more. The main benefit is realising that the ski will turn for us, if we let it. Like a train running on a banked-up track, the ski will take us round. The route has already been decided for us, we're merely a passenger on a thrilling ride!

For the technically minded: do you notice how in playing the 'commitment side-step' we are creating a new force? The moment that top ski hits the snow we cut across the line of momentum our body was following. We create a force, the force reverses the camber of the ski and produces the arc of our turning circle. By now the steering really is out of our hands. Any attempt of the body to interfere will create problems further along the line!

As I've said before, there are no rules about the right or wrong ways to do this game. Regard it as another tool in your kitbag of learning and use it in any way you wish.

SKIING IN 'BAD' LIGHT

One of my pupils told me he couldn't ski when the sun was shining because he had a sensitive skin and he was only happy when it was dull and cloudy! Most people, though, hate poor visibility – they stiffen up and their skiing goes to pieces.

Fog, white-outs, and 'bad' visibility do not, and cannot, have the power to spoil our enjoyment or interfere with our performance. After all fog, is just fog, totally unaware of your opinion and judgement about it! It is our *attitude* to the conditions which affects our performance. If we choose to be upset at the weather our skiing may quickly deteriorate and with ample justification: "It's the weather making me ski like this!"

When you are skiing in poor visibility which game do *you* play? Skiing but wishing it was clear and fine, or skiing in limited visibility but with total awareness of all

SOME 'BAD LIGHT' GAMES

1 Imagine you have got a bright searchlight shining from each knee. Look where the beam is pointing, see what you can pick up in the imaginary pool of light, follow it wherever you ski. What colour is your light and how bright is the beam?

2 Imagine your eyes were no longer in your head but in your knees. What can you see? 'Look' through your knees as you ski. Do you get quite a different view of the terrain – a better one maybe as you are closer to it now!

3 Look around you as you ski and notice what you *can* see. It's so easy to dismiss it all by saying "I can't see a thing" but look at what you *can* see – and see the difference!

4 Focus on the knees as you ski. Marvel at the constant flexing they are performing to absorb every surprise bump and mogul. Imagine your knees are the suspension on a motor-bike. Feel how they absorb every shock.

On our courses we welcome one foggy day at least. It's an invaluable learning experience!

that you can see and feel? The first game you can never win unless the sun miraculously comes out. The second game can be rewarding and enjoyable.

There *are* advantages to skiing in poor visibility!

- As your vision decreases so your sense of feeling increases as if to compensate. As skiing is a 'feeling' sport much more than a 'seeing' one our performance can often benefit and learning nearly always increases.

- As your field of vision becomes limited you are less likely to have preconceptions of the steepness of the slope ahead. You are forced to take it 'one bump at a time' thus keeping your focus of attention entirely on the 'now' and away from the future.

SUMMING UP THE THIRD DAY'S SKIING

Much of today's exercises have been about choice. You can choose to ski or not to ski! You can choose the slope, the time, the weather, the speed, the risk. You can choose the effect external conditions have on you. You can even choose your enjoyment, your learning and your performance. You can choose and create your own reality! As difficult and as controversial as this may sound, ski as if you believe it – and notice the difference.

Fourth Day

Today we are going to stretch ourselves both physically and mentally, by using our imaginations. By acting or pretending to be an animal or person who has qualities we would like to have in our skiing, we can discover and express these qualities for ourselves.

Later we shall tackle skiing moguls, and also look at our 'internal timing' to develop a rhythm for our turns.

I sometimes ask my class, "If you could ski as you would like to, how would it feel?" They reply with words like "balanced", "powerful", "relaxed" and "flowing". I ask them to choose something or someone which to them exemplifies the quality they have chosen. The choice is

ME JANE!

boundless. Some want to be "cat-like", thinking of balance and quietness. Others choose an eagle, to represent power without effort. A tiger running through the bush, a snake making smooth turns, a river flowing through fields, a butterfly floating on the breeze, a willow-tree being buffeted by winds, are all popular images.

When they have their image clear in their minds I ask them to ski in that image, to be the thing or animal they imagine. The quality they want in their skiing comes out immediately. The body provides the technique to make it possible; it is *never* the other way round.

GO GORILLA!

The more completely you enter into the role you are acting, the more you will learn and the more fun it will be. Give up skiing, become a gorilla and ham it up! The 'gorilla' game is always a success as it is so absurd; but it has to be admitted a gorilla and a balanced skier seem to have a lot in common.

So let your arms dangle to the ground – carry a bunch of bananas under one arm if you must – scream and roar of course, and ski like you've never skied before!

At the end of the run, with the slopes full of incredulous people staring after you, take a moment to consider what felt different. Check through the 'gorilla' body position and compare it with your usual effort. The arms, the shoulder blades and shoulders, the trunk and the knees may all have felt different. What characteristics would you like to keep in your skiing? Did you feel more balanced than usual? Did you notice where your weight was over your feet?

On a subconscious level the body is learning what feels 'right' automatically whenever you 'image' an animal or whatever. On a conscious level you can increase your awareness around specific actions of the body and incorporate those elements you like into your 'normal' skiing.

SING OUT WHILE YOU SKI!

Most people ski earnestly and silently. 'Let go' and discard the earnestness by expressing yourself verbally. Give a few shouts, an occasional "yippee" or imitate the call of the animal you are 'imaging'. It helps to get you deeper into the role, gets you further away from just being you and certainly gets rid of any tensions.

Singing a song works too – as long as you sing it at the top of your voice!

If you can keep going as you ski past someone standing staring at you on the piste, you have gone a long way towards 'letting go'. After that, skiing is pretty easy really!

THE 'IMAGE' GAME

1 Choose the quality you desire in your skiing and the animal or object that best represents it.

2 Ski keeping the image clearly in focus, just 'being' that image.

3 Try this game with your companions; see if you can guess the image your companions have chosen from the way they are skiing, and then see if they can guess yours. You can often guess quite accurately, which emphasises the body's apparent reaction to a clearly held image.

4 Be aware of how your body is feeling. Is it more relaxed, more balanced, more flowing? How much of you is being your 'image'? If you are being a cat, is *all* of you a cat or is part of you feeling foolish or wishing you had chosen another image?

Once you are a cat, a bird, a tree or a rushing stream you are no longer a skier struggling down a slope. The 'trying' syndrome diminishes as the qualities you want appear. I know someone who whenever he's not happy about his skiing, asks himself "Now, how would our cat ski this slope?" His arms reach forward, his weight moves over towards the balls of his feet, his shoulders relax, and he looks ahead. "Ah, of course!" he says, and gets on with the run!

POLE PLANTING

The pole-plant provides the skier with timing and rhythm. It is the trigger for the turn which follows. By staying totally focussed on the 'present', or the moment the pole hits the snow, you are less likely to be distracted by thoughts about the past (the last turn) or the future (the next turn).

Peak awareness is at its most effective at the instant of action, and the pole-plant provides an easily definable 'moment in time'.

THE 'PLOP' OF YOUR POLE-PLANT

1 Create an image for your pole-plant which will make it easier to keep your attention on it. I like to imagine the basket of the pole is like a dragon-fly landing gently on to the surface of a pond. Alternatively you can act the part of a park-keeper picking up litter on a spike.

2 Plant the pole beside you where it feels most natural and comfortable, and say the word "plop" as it hits the snow. Choose a word more appropriate to the action if "plop" doesn't go with your image!

3 The game is to keep the timing accurate so that you are saying "plop" **precisely** at the moment of impact. Not as easy as it sounds, but very absorbing and relaxing when you get your internal timing corresponding with your skiing.

4 Ask a friend to follow you to check whether your timing is as accurate as you think it is!

5 Two ways to increase the accuracy are to slow the action of the pole-plant down to slow-motion speed, and to look at the point of impact with the snow.

6 Notice the point in the snow (in relation to your lower ski) where you are planting the pole. Is it the same on left and right turns?

7 When one wrist is planting the pole, what is happening to the other? Can you feel a 'marching' motion developing, with each pole either approaching or retreating from its point of planting?

This is a relaxing and absorbing exercise, excellent for cutting out external and internal distraction. Best of all, it creates an awareness of your internal timing with which all your skiing actions must harmonise.

HOLD ON TO THE BABY BIRDS!

When your shoulders and arms are feeling tense and stiff here's an exercise which can release those tensions immediately!

1 Imagine that you have found two tiny fledgling birds that have fallen out of their nest.

2 Pick them up, one in each hand, as if to carry them to safety. Hold them firmly enough so they don't escape, but not so tightly that you crush them to death!

3 Now ski the rest of the run with them held in your hand. Notice whether you do squeeze one suddenly, or even let go! You'll feel your ski poles nestling in your grip and you'll be aware of any tension in your back or shoulders as soon as it starts. Awareness alone can bring change in the form of a more relaxed body, as this exercise will prove.

SKIING THE BUMPS

Which of the following statements do you agree with?

- "Mogul skiing is very difficult, sometimes frightening and if you fall you can slide a long way. It needs more sophisticated technique, and I'm not good enough to handle moguls yet."

                          OR

- "Moguls offer more challenges, more tests to my ability to balance and to react spontaneously to the changing terrain. I enjoy selecting the route through the moguls which feels most comfortable for me, and trusting my body and skis to perform as they have already proved they can on other slopes."

Your perception of a slope of moguls is going to dictate how successfully you ski that slope. It's the same problem as your attitude to bad visibility which we discussed on Day 3. A mogul slope is 'nasty' and 'vicious' and has to be attacked and fought; or a mogul slope has become a mogul slope because the many people who have skied it created the bumps, making it a more interesting challenge!

Technique and all that!

This section, read separately, is not going to give you the answers to skiing moguls. All the techniques which your body has learned whilst doing the exercises in this book will be needed. There is no such thing as 'mogul technique'! What you need you already have, if you've explored the drills and exercises so far:

1 A clear perception of the slope, the bumps, their size and location.

2 Absolute trust in your skis to take you along the route you select.

3 Trust in your body to produce whatever technique is required to handle the extra challenges of the bumps.

4 A commitment to skiing the slope and route you have chosen. There are other slopes and other routes down. The choice is yours but you need to make it.

5 Perhaps a target of the number of turns you are going to make, or the point you intend reaching before you stop.

If you have all of these, only your strength will limit how far you can ski and enjoy it!

A look at the slope

Come with me to a mogul slope and let's see what we can see.

1 Do you notice that each mogul, though different, has similar characteristics? On the downhill side they are steep, smooth and icy, and on the uphill side they have much more loose snow.

2 How steep do you think the slope is? Hold your pole at the angle of slope and then check. Now you have a more accurate representation. Compare it with your emotional perception of the degree of slope!

3 Imagine a stream flowing past your feet down the slope. If it was meandering lazily what route would it take? Now let it flow faster until it's a torrent, check the routes and see the differences.

4 Notice where the stream is turned by the bumps, watching how it rises up the side of the bump before descending down into the channel between them.

5 When we ski the slope we're going to select one of the routes the stream would take. Look for the 'banking' where the stream changes direction and enjoy the thrill of 'riding up the sides' in defiance of gravity. This for me is the game of skiing bumps – choosing your line. The embankments give you the thrill of turning, and searching out these embankments produces the line of your run.

6 When you've seen a route, decide how many turns you want to make. If the whole slope looks endless, take it in sections, making perhaps just three turns and stopping. By dividing the whole slope into manageable chunks you get the feel of linking turns and achieving results.

If you ever thought you had to give your body instructions before it could ski, a mogul slope is the best place to dispel that theory. There is no time! Bump skiing is reaction skiing, with the body absorbing all the forces of gravity, momentum and immovable objects acting on it.

Have fun in the moguls

Here are some games to play which will help make the moguls more fun.

THE WILLOW TREE

This exercise in imagery I find very powerful on mogul slopes.

1 Before you start off down the slope, close your eyes for a moment and imagine yourself to be a willow tree. Feel your 'roots' firmly planted in the ground, your 'branches' dangling, your 'trunk' swaying gently in the 'breeze'.

2 Stay with the image as you open your eyes and start to ski. The moguls may be big and put you off your balance, the slope may be icy and steep, but your willow tree can be buffeted by the fiercest winds, bending this way and that, without ever being uprooted!

3 Become aware of your 'centre'. Feel the energy from your centre flowing down to your roots keeping you stable and balanced and able to counter the forces which seem to want to knock you over.

SKI LIKE A CHILD

Children ski with their legs wide apart; let's ski like them. Look for the outside ski riding up around the banked turns.

POP THE BALLOONS

A natural way to find a flowing route through the moguls is to 'pop the balloons'!

1 Imagine that on top of every mogul is a brightly coloured balloon.

2 As you ski past each balloon, 'pop' it with your ski pole. The more balloons you manage to pop, the more direct your route will be.

3 Look at the balloon as you pop it – make sure you get it right in the middle!

4 Say the word 'pop' as your pole explodes the balloon.

Though it sounds more akin to a child's party game, notice the difference when your attention is totally focussed on the 'now' of the pop.

Feel the route your skis are taking around the moguls producing an efficient line almost automatically. I recommend popping balloons on obstacles like rocks and ice patches too.

THE MAGNET UNDER YOUR SKIS

The more ski edge which is in contact with the snow in moguls the more control you will enjoy and the smoother your line. The 'magnet' game is easy to play and can be instantly effective.

1 Imagine a magnet under the front of both of your skis pulling them towards the ground.

2 As you ski around or over moguls feel the front of the ski be 'attracted' to the snow every time it loses contact.

It's as simple as that; and you'll enjoy the feeling of your edges keeping you on track throughout the turn.

THE CHANGING RHYTHM

Plenty of skiers can ski moguls fast. How about slow-motion skiing? How slowly can you ski five consecutive turns?

Many of the exercises, drills and games we've looked at together in this book are just as valuable to you on the bumps. Any difference lies in your attitude to the slope. So try some of the exercises you have found helpful earlier in the week.

Looking for your route, playing some of these games and breaking the slope down into easily handled sections can take the fear out of mogul skiing and put the thrill back in!

DOWNHILL SKIING IS A 'SILLY' GAME

Downhill skiing is a simple pursuit with little purpose other than to thrill and excite. We experience it best when we bring to it a child-like joy and enthusiasm, and like children live for the moment with yesterday forgotten and tomorrow never thought of. Experiencing the fun leaves no room for judging your performance, comparing yourself with others or trying to 'get it right'.

The basic fun and joy of the 'silly game' of skiing are lost if you take it all too seriously. Those who bring to it earnestness, persistence and occasional despair begin to play another game, a much sillier game, one they can rarely win. Those who discover the magic of the real game of skiing are those who let go of their adult pose or act and play the game as children play it – naturally.

SUMMING UP THE FOURTH DAY'S SKIING

After four days of the programme how do you feel about your skiing? Are you on course for getting what you want out of the week? If not, what's getting in the way?

Do you want to realign your objectives and perhaps choose those you feel most committed to achieving in the next two days? Have you been doing precisely and exclusively what the exercise suggests you do, or have you been looking for a particular result and perhaps blocking the opportunity of other results appearing?

Most importantly, are you enjoying your skiing?

Remember the power of imagery, introduced today and to be explored in greater depth on the last day. There is nothing you cannot improve on when you bring in your imagination.

Fifth Day

Today we are going to look at our balance and control. Many skiers rate 'being in control' as their main objective in their skiing.

It's not difficult to be in control – you just grit your teeth, stiffen your legs and snow-plough everywhere. You can keep upright all day on and off-piste. You won't have enjoyed it very much, but you will have been in control!

Controlled skiing is a paradox. You achieve it when you let go of it – hang on to it, and you'll never get there. Today's exercises and games should help.

The ski boot of today is unrecognisable compared with the boot of the 1960's and before. The improvement in design has been the single biggest contribution to making skiing a safe and easy-to-learn sport. Skis and safety bindings too are continually being improved, but it is the boot alone that provides the link or communication between you and the snow. Today's boots clamp the whole foot and ankle in what feels like a solid cocoon. The only movement allowed is forward flex of the ankle. There is no sideways movement at all, thanks to the stiffness of the modern materials used in their construction. You can even adjust the canting of the boot to compensate for a skier's inclination to bow-leggedness or knock-knees! Apart from greater comfort the skier has more precision over the edging of his skis. Any sideways movement of the leg is transmitted directly to the ski edge and is not absorbed by a flimsy leather boot, a foot bandage and two pairs of old sailing socks (that's what I had to put up with when I began skiing)!

Boot designers may have been influenced by the traditional ski teachers. Recognising the value of flexible knees whilst skiing, instructors tell you to bend your knees. Boot manufacturers go one better and now don't allow you to straighten your leg! Instructors have been heard to tell pupils to lean back and get the ski tips above the snow in powder – so the manufacturers follow up with reinforced high backs which you can virtually

lean back against. Your boot is not going to ski for you, however the design tries to mould you into someone's idea of an 'appropriate' position. A boot cannot hold you up in a balanced position (well, maybe in the shop, but

not when you are moving). It will, however, *support* your balanced position and give you optimum effectiveness *from* that position. Do you understand the difference?

Look around you on the mountain. So many people are skiing *with* their boots not *in* their boots. They are not balanced. Their boots are holding them up, usually preventing them from falling over backwards!

How balanced are **you** in your boots? There is one easy way to find out!

UNDO THOSE BOOTS!

1 Choose a modest slope.

2 Undo the top clips of your boot – usually the first two, but keep one done up to keep yourself attached to your skis!

3 Now your ankle has total freedom forwards and backwards, and some movement sideways too.

4 Start to ski, gently at first, but doing anything you feel confident to do.

5 Notice how your foot is working to keep you balanced. From the toes to the heel the muscles and bones are very active, feeling the snow and the skis, and responding to this input. What does it feel like? It's not easy at first, is it? Let the body find its balanced position.

6 How is your skiing? The value of this experiment lies in the problem! If you can't turn, feel unstable or don't want to carry on, ask yourself why. What are you doing to prevent yourself from standing in a balanced position? You know you don't **need** your boots to balance you, so without the benefit of their support what's getting in the way?

7 Are you reading the snow with your feet? It is much easier without the constriction of tight boots.

8 Stay with it a little longer. Years ago people skied well in boots little better than bedroom slippers. Here's your chance to discover the balance, feel and sensitivity that they enjoyed.

With a little practice you'll be able to ski quite naturally. When you do your boots up again the lessons you've just learnt will help you put your boots into a different context. They are designed to support the natural movement of the leg, not immobilise and replace it!

Many pupils find this exercise is amazingly effective and immediately benefit from it. Why should one 'drill' be more effective than another? The reason is that when your boots are undone, you are committed 100 per cent to the exercise – you have no choice! So this game teaches the value of commitment, too.

SKIING WITH YOUR EYES SHUT

As if skiing wasn't difficult enough already, now I'm going to ask you to close your eyes while you do it! Blotting out the visual input will help you focus on the feeling in your feet and legs. With our eyes closed we can marvel at the many subtle and intricate muscle movements in our feet and legs that are continually taking place. We cannot see where we are, so we know that it's not 'us' instructing these movements, it's the body being allowed to perform what needs to be done unhindered by advice and directions from our egos!

This lesson is always brought home to me when skiing in fog or a white-out. Sometimes you cannot even see if you're going uphill or down, and you certainly can't distinguish bumps. Yet when you focus attention on your legs they are humming with activity – absorbing the contours, telling you what sort of snow you are on and directing your course.

Let's experience some of this learning from the next exercise – and it can be fun too!

SKIING BLIND

1 Choose a quiet part of the piste; you must have a companion with you for this one to watch out for your safety.

2 When you know it is safe to go, have a look ahead, close your eyes, and slowly proceed.

3 At first you may feel tension in your feet as you back away from the unknown. If you do, open your eyes to reassure yourself, close them again and continue.

4 Apart from the sounds you can hear, you are relying entirely for information on the messages fed to you by your legs. What are they telling you? What's going on? Are you turning to the left and right without difficulty?

5 Have you noticed the position of your skis? Are they further apart than usual? Do you feel more or less balanced than usual? Do you feel your legs acting independently?

6 Ask your companion to ski behind you guiding you down the hill telling you to turn where it's appropriate and safe. Then reverse the roles! Again, the trust element in skiing is important. If you are not able to trust your companion to guide you, choose another one!

7 What are the lessons for you in skiing with your eyes shut? Our eyes give us a perception of a slope: its steepness, its dangers, its problems. Our perception creates fear, anxiety and tension if the difficulties are magnified. With our eyes closed we have fewer perceptions. For once our body has more of a chance of just getting on with the job!

THE HUMAN VIDEO

In so many of the exercises and games we use, the value comes from an unexpected quarter. This is essentially true when playing 'the Human Video'.

1 Ski in pairs a few metres apart, one behind the other. The skier in front skis the slope normally whilst the skier following mimics their movements. I ask my group to pretend they are extras in a film and they are going to have to 'stand-in' for the star they are following, and have to look exactly like them.

2 It takes a little while to copy someone else's mannerisms and style. Start by selecting one aspect of their skiing, rather like a caricaturist might, and copy just this, even exaggerating it a little. They might have a particular way of planting their pole so copy it until you can do it the same. Then find another characteristic. Perhaps the head nods from side to side! After skiing behind them for a few hundred metres you will almost be a carbon copy. Now overtake and ski in front, keeping the same style. They can now see what they look like; just like a video.

3 "But he doesn't ski as well as I do, copying him is going to destroy my skiing!" You are only acting. An actor mimicking a foreign accent in a play reverts easily to his normal voice off-stage. To give your companion the best value in this exercise you are going to have to act very well.

4 If you are the one who is being copied you can pick up traits you might not have noticed otherwise, and at the very least it will raise your awareness of them.

5 It is easy to select only the 'faults' and copy those, but try to absorb and reproduce the whole image the other skier presents.

6 You may be horrified by some characteristic shown you by the 'human video'. But it has been brought to your attention (the starting point for all change) and you can safely assume that your companion was exaggerating to make the point, so don't be too disheartened!

7 And now for the most valuable results of the game:

"I don't usually ski as fast as that on this sort of slope."

"I've never done so many turns on one run."

"I was so relaxed, not even noticing where I was going."

"I've never skied so well."

These are typical of the comments I receive from those who were (surprise, surprise) doing the copying, providing the 'human video'. They joined in the experiment assuming that the results were all aimed at the person being copied. With no expectations, no looking for results, they are amazed at the effect it has on their own skiing. Frequently, so am I!

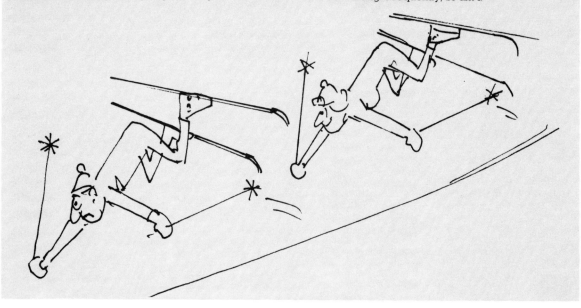

BALANCE

Nobody can teach you how to balance. You have to discover it for yourself. There is no other way! The exercises, drills and games in this section are about letting the body make the discoveries of balance itself, whilst we, and our egos, keep out of the way.

How our 'ego' interferes with our balance

Most of our lives we spend walking on flat ground with plenty of friction between our feet and the surface we are on. I call the balance needed for this 'static balance', and by now we are really pretty good at it!

Skiing however presents a different challenge to our ability to balance. There is forward movement and speed, and there is little friction between us and the surface we are skiing on. The balance we require for this I call 'dynamic balance'.

One of the balancing factors which keep you upright on skis is the body's response to an external force, or pull, which you can only experience when you are actually moving.

Do you remember the experiment we tried on the children's roundabout? We let go of the hand-rail and let the body lean away from the pull which was trying to throw us off the roundabout: that was 'dynamic balance'! You couldn't have stayed in that position with the roundabout stopped, because the support you were leaning against (the pull to the outside) would no longer be there.

So you cannot practise dynamic balance whilst standing still, you will just fall over! You also cannot practise static balance whilst you are skiing without experiencing the awkwardness and loss of mobility which must accompany it.

You can see what I'm talking about on the slopes all the time – I call it the 'Chancery Lane walk' after one of our pupils who had an office in Chancery Lane, London. I can imagine him striding to the office each morning, his head up, shoulders back, chest out, looking immaculate, confident and smart. A picture of efficiency and success, complete with furled umbrella. Others stop to watch him with admiration as he confidently takes his place for another day in the rat-race of the city. A winner through and through!

On the slopes he applies the same rules which work for him so well elsewhere. Head up, chest out, shoulders back, bottom out and. . . crash!

Do you see what I mean about the difference between the balance you need for walking, and the balance you need for skiing? What the difference is does not matter. Recognising that there **is** a difference is fundamental to our progress as skiers. We will then be free to discover the balance we need for ourselves.

The exercises and drills that follow are all designed to allow your body to 'discover' balance. The extent to which you find them interesting, absorbing or effective is the extent to which you will 'block out' the irrelevant advice from your 'little voice'.

Balance equals trust. Off-balance equals lack of trust. Put another way, our ability to be balanced equals our potential to balance minus the lack of trust in our body's ability to find the balance.

Let's discover **our** potential to balance.

Discovering our centre

We all have a centre of gravity – the point in our body which represents our very middle, our centre. Height and weight differences mean that for each of us it's in a different place and usually, with age, we discover our centres getting lower and lower! As a rough guide it is two or three centimetres below our navel and then in a bit. When our centre is out of balance, we too are out of balance. When we are out of balance we tend to compensate by spontaneous and often erratic body movements, particularly in the arms. I'm sure you've seen what I mean!

Awareness brings change

Instead of trying to work out where our centre 'should' be, let's be clear where it **is** as we ski. As we've seen before with so many of the drills we've done together, awareness brings change. When the feedback tells the body where your centre is, adjustments will be made automatically to let your centre find the optimum point of balance at all times.

FINDING YOUR CENTRE

1 Ski with one hand pressed lightly against you where you gauge your centre to be.

2 Keep the same hand in place all the time helping to keep you constantly aware of your centre and where it is at all times. It's a simple exercise but, almost as if by magic, a change to greater balance will follow.

3 What was your experience of doing this? Did you feel calmer, more relaxed? Did you miss not being able to use your ski pole on one side?

SEARCHLIGHTS!

1 Imagine you've got a huge searchlight strapped to your waist pointing out straight ahead of you.

2 Before you start to ski, switch on the beam, with the imaginary switch! Move the 'beam' with your body, shining it around you and straight ahead, up to the sky and down on the ground between your skis. Your beam's working OK? Is it on full power? What colour is it?

3 As you ski look at what the beam of the searchlight is picking up. A mountain peak ahead, a pylon, trees, other skiers, your own ski tips? Keep your eyes on the spot where the beam is shining.

4 There are no rules as to where you should be shining it: the feedback from where the beam is shining tells the body where your centre is.

5 Can you visualise your searchlight? Can you stay with the beam as you ski or do you lose the beam during your turns? During the turns your 'little voice' is at its loudest – after all, there is more to think about then! When you follow the searchlight beam throughout a turn the ego, absorbed by the job of following the beam, lets the turn happen without interruption. To have that experience ski more slowly until you can stay with the beam, and then later speed up.

The searchlight game has amazing results which will always be your own. When I play this game on moguls I find it has the effect of slowing the turn down whilst I survey the mountain peaks across the valley picked up by my searchlight!

I can generally guess when one of our pupils is practising the searchlight game. They have a distant look in their eye and a very quiet upper body!

THE SHOULDER-BLADE DRILL

Skiers rarely consider their shoulder blades. When they ski the position of the shoulder blades says a lot about tension in their upper body. Again, there is no **correct** place to keep your shoulder blades but you see many skiers with their blades kept rigidly in one position. Reducing tension frees them to help in balancing you dynamically.

1 Test the range of the movement. Imagine there is a walnut between your shoulder blades and you are determined to crack it open. Then open the blades to drop the walnut and continue to open them as far as you can. Ski in all these positions and notice the effect that the position of your shoulder blades has on the rest of your body. Can you see how easy it is to restrict freedom of movement and flow?

2 Remember when we imagined being a cat in the last exercise? Try it again imagining how it would feel if you were a cat poised to spring, ready to respond to danger or to absorb the shock of a sudden movement. Ready? Where are your shoulder blades now?

3 Keep the image of the cat in mind as you ski. Check your shoulder blades – are they different from their usual position? Do you feel more comfortable, more able to absorb the sudden surprises of the snow and respond to sudden changes in direction?

Where should my shoulder blades be?

Often I'm asked, "Where should my shoulder blades be?" If you've read this far into the book you'll know better than to ask! If after you have done all the exercises and become totally aware of where your shoulder blades are, and yet you still want to know, look at other skiers – particularly slalom racers. Try out for yourself what you see in others you admire. Don't however fall into the trap of making what you see in others into a rule for yourself. Instead, widen your own learning experience by copying what you see in others. You will neither copy it exactly nor will what they are doing be appropriate for you. That's not the point. Experimenting with what you see others doing, if you regard it as another learning experience, is always valuable practice.

TAKE A LOOK AT YOUR PELVIS

You may never have thought about your pelvis before, but it's always been there, working for you as a vital part of the balancing process. It can also work against you.

The pelvis is one of those areas of the body which, because of its ability to rock freely forwards and backwards when the body is relaxed, is one of the first to behave inappropriately when the body is under tension.

Increasing your awareness of where your pelvis is will free it to help you balance.

1 Go back to the searchlight exercise. Shine your beam up into the sky, straight ahead or down between your skis. If you can do that without leaning backwards or forwards you will be aware of the full movement of your pelvis.

2 Notice where your pelvis is during the whole of a run. Is it mostly forwards, in the middle or back? Feel the effect that rocking your pelvis has on your bottom. Stick your bottom out, then tuck it in. Which feels more comfortable?

3 Notice the effect that rocking your pelvis has on the lower part of the spine. Do you ever have pain in the lower part of your back? Straightening the lower spine may relieve it.

4 Focus next on the elbows. Move them forward so they are ahead of your body, then bring them right back behind you. What effect does this have on your pelvis?

5 One of my favourite imaginary exercises is to pretend to be a cat (we looked at this exercise on Day 4). Why not have a go now? Stand on a quiet part of the slope and close your eyes. Imagine you are a cat, prowling through a garden, constantly on your guard for the neighbour's fierce dog. You are looking for food but always aware of danger as you peer around you, poised for flight or fight. Any second now! You'll have to act fast!

Have you got that image of the cat? How has your physical body position changed? Is your weight over your toes, your hands ahead of you, your knees flexed?

And your pelvis? Be aware of that position. Do you see the difference between that and how you normally stand? That's dynamic balance!

Fear seems to block the free rocking ability of the pelvis. When I ask pupils to be aware of their pelvis it immediately relaxes and they let it rock to the appropriate position. Rigid pelvises are the most common symptom of anxiety on the mountain. By making a game out of watching where the pelvis is, or where the 'beam' is shining, you help change the attitude producing the anxiety and free the 'blockage' at the same time!

HANG ON TO YOUR HULA HOOP!

For this inspired image I am indebted to John Sheddon and his excellent book *Skilful Skiing*.

1 Imagine you are in the middle of a hula hoop. It's a light one, made of plastic perhaps and brightly coloured. What colour have you chosen? Hold it wherever feels comfortable and let's go for a ski.

2 Do you feel silly holding on to a hula hoop? No one can see it – and if anybody stops to watch, it will only be to admire your balanced position!

3 Notice where your hands are holding the hula hoop – in front of you, at the side or behind you? I'd like you to ski with your hands in all these positions to feel the effect on your balance. Notice the shoulder blades!

4 How tightly are you gripping the hula hoop? Are you hanging on to it as if your life depended upon it, or are you letting it rest in your lightly closed hand?

5 Watch when your grip suddenly tightens, or when you let go altogether. Don't try and avoid these things happening but just notice them! When you let go, quickly reach for the hula hoop and regain your balance.

6 Look at the slalom racers on TV, or the good skiers on the slopes. Can you see their hula hoop? Can you see too when they let go of it – and then catch it again?

7 I'd like you to notice two qualities in your hula hoop: its diameter increases and decreases, and it can move freely up and down your body. Play around with these variables, finding positions which seem natural for balance.

8 In difficult snow, powder or steep moguls try keeping the hula hoop as low as you can – say around the top of your boots. After a couple of turns you may realize that it has come up of its own accord as you naturally discover the comfortable position.

9 Ask a companion to watch your hula hoop and then compare where **he** saw it with where **you** thought it was. You'll be amazed at the difference!

10 Watch to see the levelness of the hoop. Are your eyes and the hula hoop always horizontal?

Holding a hula hoop does have the most amazing effects on skiers. Not only does it instantly create a flowing, balanced feel and look, but it acts as a support in times of crisis and as a tool to provide valuable feedback.

Next time you're standing nervously on top of a mogul slope, take hold of your hula hoop first and then go for it! Like the racers you'll discover it's a vital part of your ski equipment.

SOME MORE BALANCING EXERCISES

The next four exercises have two things in common. One is that in doing them you really begin to appreciate that you cannot tell the body how to balance, but that you have to let it do it itself. The other is perhaps the key to the Ski Skills approach and everything we've been looking at together. I won't spoil it for you by describing it now. Let's wait until the end.

FLOATING THE INSIDE SKI

1 Pretend your inside ski is like the outrigger of a canoe. Its job is to balance the craft, help absorb unexpected waves and to assist stability. When the canoe is in perfect trim it rides above the water level just skimming the surface, there if needed but not impeding the momentum of the boat.

2 Imagine your inside ski is acting as your outrigger. Feel it skimming across the snow barely disturbing the surface, almost weightless, floating.

3 Have you got the feeling of it floating? It's not the same as picking it up altogether, which would feel heavy. Can you hear it when it's floating? A quiet hum interspersed with occasional crackles as it hits a ripple of snow!

4 If you find it difficult to float that ski, stop for a minute and get a companion to pull on your downhill ski stick to simulate the pull on your body during a turn. Now let the top ski (the inside ski) 'float'. No problems there? If you find it's more difficult to do when you are moving, ask yourself if you are concentrating on your skiing so that you can do the exercise, or are you just concentrating on the exercise and letting the skiing get on by itself.

5 When we've become accustomed to floating the ski let's take it further and refine the feedback even more. At what point in the turn does the inside ski begin to float? At the beginning, in the middle or at the end when the turn is safely over? When you've picked up the point at which it begins to float, see if you can make it earlier and earlier. See if you can aim to start it floating at the very start of a turn!

6 Find the point at which the inside ski has given up its floating role and the other ski has not yet taken it over. How long is the changeover? Does it need to be any longer than an instant? Explore reducing this time, and then increasing it.

FLOATING THE OUTSIDE SKI

A valuable exercise to test your balance. There's no physical reason why we cannot do this easily but you will find it seems strange at first. When you can do this you will fully appreciate the amazing balancing and recovery properties of the body. Skills you will be using a lot in moguls and more challenging skiing!.

FLOATING THE HEEL OF THE INSIDE SKI

1 Imagine a balloon filled with helium under the back of your inside ski. With the toe still skimming the surface the heel is being supported gently on a cushion of air. Notice a change in body position immediately you have this image – the body wastes no time in adapting. How balanced do you feel now as you ski with this new image?

2 Notice the effect this new image has, if any, on the big toe of the other foot.

3 Now go back to the original exercise of floating the inside ski. Is that easier?

PUMPING UP THE CAR TYRE

1 Imagine that with your inside ski you are operating a foot-pump to inflate a car tyre. Pressing down with your toe you raise and lower your heel to work the pump.

2 As you ski, start pumping! Pay attention to the rhythm you are choosing. Is it a steady beat or always varying? Try it faster and then slower.

3 When you've established a rhythm see if you can get the next ski to take it over without disrupting the beat. Not easy at first, but when you can do it you will know how it feels to be totally balanced all the time.

4 The acid test: have a go at pumping with the outside ski. It's the ultimate in feedback as to whether you are 'on your skis'!

Where is the learning in these exercises? It is in discovering whether you are balanced on your skis. If you are not these drills will be very awkward to do, and you are consciously or subconsciously interfering with your body's balancing ability.

And there's a bonus!

So what was the feature of these balancing exercises that I wouldn't describe at the beginning? It was that they very clearly 'fool' our ego. The interference which we experience so often is not, for a change, being directed at the mechanics of our skiing. The ego is so absorbed in the challenge of 'floating a ski' or 'pumping a tyre' that the operation of skiing is almost completely neglected. The body is left to sort out the skiing for itself. The effort, self-criticism and instruction which our ego introduces is wholly concentrated on something which has little to do with our skiing.

How deeply did you concentrate on performing these drills well? The degree of concentration indicates the degree to which the body could ski unhindered, with no tension, awkwardness or effort.

How did it feel? Have you discovered how **you** can get in the way of your own balancing?

All skiing is about the skill of balancing. I hope after you've done today's exercises you will discover you already have this skill – in abundance!

BALANCING – A CASE HISTORY

One pupil in my group recently was a girl in her twenties who skied confidently and loved the off-piste. She was the best skier in this particular group and was aware of and flattered by the attention her skiing received. She wanted greater control in difficult conditions and to feel less tired after a long run. She skied in a very definite 'style' which could only have been achieved after years of practice.

She wanted me to watch her skiing in the off-piste and to tell her 'her faults' so she could practise eliminating them. Though her technique was straight from a text-book it was constantly interfering with her natural ability to balance. She said she had all the balance in the world, she just lacked technique in difficult conditions! It looked to me as if she couldn't express her ability to balance, and that she was relying on technique to replace trust.

She was very reluctant and sceptical when I suggested we explore balance on a nursery slope. She hadn't skied on one of those for years!

I asked her to do the 'foot pump' drill, and to her utter amazement she found her foot locked solid, unable to move. Whilst others in the class were happily doing the

drill, she was unable to give up the very 'technique' which was blocking her balance. She recognised the 'blockage' and we spent two more days exploring the learning that comes from trusting the body to achieve what you want.

The next time we were off-piste the difference was dramatic. She looked and felt solid and balanced. This time she was unaware of the attention she was creating; the skiing was much more fun!

THE LEVEL OF YOUR EYES

Look around you at the other skiers. Look at the level of their eyes. It tells you a great deal about not only their skiing, but sometimes what they are thinking about as they ski. And that's with goggles on! Let's look at some different types:

1 The "I'm checking out the ends of my skis" type. He likes his new skis so much he can't take his eyes off them. Not for a minute. Perhaps he keeps them by his bed so he can gaze at them at night too! Do you stare down at the pavement just in front of you continually as you walk?

2 The "I must look down the mountain at all times" type. He's very common. Way back in his skiing career someone taught him that whatever he did, wherever he went, he must look down the mountain.

3 A variation of (2) is "I'm looking down the mountain and aren't I looking good too?" This species is much photographed and still occasionally features on the covers of tour operators' brochures. They are dying out but imitators abound to ensure that their demise is slow and lingering!

4 "Noddy." Head and eyes rock from side to side. This type is relaxed, and contentedly skis oblivious to all others.

5 The "I'm just a little nervous of this slope" type. A fixed stare and no movement at all!

From the comfort of your chair-lift you can see these types and more as you go up for your next run. Look too for the skiers who are creating a 'flowing' image, who appear calm and relaxed; notice the line made by their eyes and see if you can spot any similarities they have, and any differences with the other skiers on the mountain.

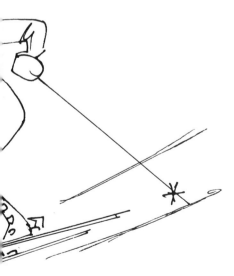

CHECK YOUR EYE LEVEL

Now it's your turn! On this next run notice the line which joins your eyes. It's easy if you are wearing goggles or a hat to give you an artificial horizon. Tilt your head slowly from side to side. See your 'horizon' tilting also. That's the line we are going to concentrate on.

1 Ski for a few hundred metres just noticing the line of your horizon.

2 Watch if and when it dips to the left and to the right. Is the dip more to one side than the other?

3 Compare your turns to the left and to the right; does your horizon dip down towards the outside ski, the inside ski or stay level?

4 If you notice a change of level during the turns determine which turn has the greater degree of angle on your horizon.

5 As you ski, keep altering your horizontal 'hold'. See what it's like to ski with the level tilted to its maximum on one side, then the other. Some positions are much more comfortable than others. By testing all positions your body can learn both what it likes, and recognise when a 'forced' position is restricting your freedom to ski naturally.

6 Imagine you are piloting a private plane! In front of you above the controls you can see an instrument which tells you the trim of the plane – how level it is at all times. It's especially important to pay attention to this when coming in to land! As you ski keep the level as horizontal as you can. You may well dip down a little on both sides but gently bring it back up to the level again. Notice particularly any changes as you go through a turn and see how level you can keep it, and for how long!

When I look at this 'eye level' exercise with a group of skiers I often get comments like these:

"I had no idea my head was being so busy!"

"I've always felt strained in traversing from left to right. Now I've noticed that my head is tilted and my neck is under tension on one traverse – but not on the other."

"I had a feeling of calmness and peace and felt my skis were skiing for me."

"I didn't look down at my skis once – it felt good."

When a pilot notices that he is out of trim he doesn't

panic or feel a sense of failure. He quietly corrects and if the level goes the other way he quietly corrects again. Whilst doing this exercise adopt the same manner, quietly getting back to level each time you notice a drift away.

OUR BALANCING MECHANISM

Inside our heads is the mechanism for keeping us balanced. When our mechanism is level, balance is natural. When our mechanism is itself out of level, any corrections to the body have a built-in bias which has to be overcome before balance is regained.

Stand in front of a mirror

Try it for yourself. Stand on one leg and watch your eyes in the mirror. Now tilt your eyes slightly. Do you notice a compensating reaction in your foot? You are no longer balanced on the same part of the foot. Now realign your eyes to level again. Does that feel more comfortable?

Test it on a traverse

Find a long traverse on a reasonable slope and ski across dipping your 'eye level' down to the lower ski. Do you feel any tension in your hips? Only the position of your balancing mechanism has changed, but your hips have compensated in an unnecessary attempt to recover equilibrium. By keeping your balance mechanism level you're giving the body the best chance of keeping its balance beneath you.

Beware the trap!

Now you have discovered this for yourself, don't make it a rule. Rules inhibit freedom in your skiing. Merely notice the levelness of your horizon as you ski – you will find the correction comes automatically. If you make it a rule you will find you start forcing your body into unnatural positions.

ONE LEG OR TWO?

From early in our skiing career when we inevitably start with legs wide apart in the snow-plough position, it seems our goal is to ski with our legs closer and closer together until, ultimate of ultimates, no daylight can be seen between them.

The result is what I call the 'mermaid effect' as skiers waddle inelegantly down the hill with their arms waving and their upper-body twisting ruthlessly to stay upright whilst their legs are clamped firmly together.

If you really want to ski like that you would be much better off skiing on one ski, or better still on a mono-board where you are literally clamped into that position!

Watch the racers on TV, both slalom and downhill. Look at the amazing independent leg action they produce. In a slalom their skis are parallel for less than 20 per cent of the time and their legs together hardly at all! So much for that myth.

By keeping the legs together your body won't be allowed to ski efficiently, there will be wasted effort, and you won't be able to respond naturally to the forces acting on you as you ski.

Give me two legs every time. I feel much more stable!

Balance is never a static position!

THE BICYCLE GAME

Do you remember we looked at the joins between the constituent parts of a skier's movement? The bicycle exercise gets rid of any gaps and produces one fluid movement – just like when you are riding a bicycle.

1 Pedal down on one foot applying ever-increasing pressure, whilst allowing the pressure in the other foot to come up, as you would when riding a bicycle.

2 Pretend you are pedalling up steep hills and feel the difference.

3 Vary the speed at which you pedal and notice the difference to your skiing.

From this exercise we can make a major discovery that it seems most of the skiers we see on the mountain have yet to make: our legs are two independent units, each acting separately from the other. Each leg is responsible for absorbing the pressure applied on it by the changing terrain and the changing forces acting on you.

CHECKING YOUR OWN FOUNDATIONS

All the exercises, drills and games so far have been suggested for you to do on slopes and at speeds well within your capabilities. The safer the environment, the fewer distractions and the more learning. Naturally when your focussing-in ability increases you can take this new skill to discover what you are doing under more and more stressful conditions, faster, steeper and deeper! But until you can block out every interference and stay with what interests you, your learning will be frustrated.

Imagine you are building your own chalet in your favourite ski resort. It's nearly completed except for the roof and the finishing touches. You invite a friend who knows the area well to come and look at it. Whilst admiring its many fine qualities he points out that the foundations are poorly built and showing signs of subsidence. Now you are in a predicament. You can either go ahead and finish the roof, although you admit to yourself one of the supports is already looking out of line. Or, despite how near you felt you were to finishing, you could dismantle what you've built, keeping all the materials, re-make the foundations solid and true, and rebuild the top.

The same predicament faces skiers who want to lift their skiing off the plateau of the two-week-a-year piste-basher. You can try to adapt any learning to fit on top of the mixture of ability you've acquired to date. Or you can rebuild the foundations of your skiing from the lowest level to give you the potential of unlimited achievement.

I refer to this example frequently when I sense that fairly proficient skiers wonder why we are starting off on gentle slopes. They are always free to choose, within reason, where we shall ski, but they quickly see the point of looking at basics.

Many is the time that a good powder skier has noticed while doing snow-ploughs on a nursery slope that (say) on one turn he brings his hip round to follow his outside ski, something that he doesn't do on the other turn. He remembers that his falls off-piste are generally always to one side, the same side that he's now become aware of on the nursery slope. From this point learning is very fast and within a day we can be looking at the challenges of the off-piste with much more confidence and consistency.

The joins in the structure

We discussed earlier the syndrome of the skier who knows what he has to do to become the skier he wants to be. He's analysed every movement and indeed can often reproduce them, though not always in the right order or even when it is appropriate! Somehow you can always see the joins in the structure.

Here are four games to play that will help stop you thinking about the various complex movements you've got to make. Instead I hope you will find they are absorbing in themselves and in playing them you find the body gets on with the skiing fluidly!

CAT AND MOUSE

For two skiers of similar ability. The one in front is the 'mouse' whilst the one at the back is the 'cat' chasing it. The cat must follow exactly in the mouse's track without taking any short cuts. The cat wins if it can touch the mouse's arm. This is very exhausting for the cat, who to stay in the track of the mouse has to concentrate entirely on the mouse's skiing. The mouse has the advantage of seeing and selecting its terrain, and the cat has less time to prepare for turns. There is no time to think. For two skiers of very similar standard the mouse has a big advantage, but the cat can win!

SHADOWING

You can play this with one or a number of friends (four is about the maximum). The skier in front skis a fairly direct flowing line down the piste. The one behind shadows the leader turn for turn, staying always directly uphill from him. If he's accurate then the view from below would be of one skier only! Others can join the line taking their pace and rhythm from the one in front of them and everybody shadowing the leader. Not only must you anticipate the skier ahead so that you turn exactly at the same time as they do, but you must remember you too are being followed and copied. Two tricks I find work for me: start very slowly, and make an exaggerated slow pole-plant movement so the person behind can anticipate your turn.

You will notice that whilst the skier at the front can choose where to turn the 'shadowers' have no such choice; this provides practice in turning on terrain you would usually avoid!

FORMATION SKIING

Similar to the above exercise except you can choose a formation: a straight line across the slope like a chorus line, a V-formation, or a square with a skier at each corner. Now you have to concentrate on keeping yourself aligned with at least two other skiers, whilst also checking that the formation is keeping the original shape. A bit more difficult. I often suggest a group forms two identical formations and, if there's room, ski next to each other with another member of the group at the bottom of the hill to award marks for presentation, team-work and entertainment value!

THE LITTLE VOICE GAME

I call this the 'little voice' game because of the little voice we hear in our head as we ski – the one that says "How am I looking?" – "It's a bit steep here" – "There's a nasty icy patch ahead" – "I must keep my bottom in". This is the chance for this voice to come into its own.

Ski in pairs one ahead of the other. The one at the back is going to act the 'little voice' of the skier in front. You need to keep close behind so the first skier can hear. Your aim is to give them so many things to think and worry about that it upsets their skiing completely. The first skier's aim is to just ski and be totally unaffected by your comments!

Keep the flow of comments going – lots of judgements and criticism, praise, instruction, advice, warnings about the snow conditions, pointing out the people looking at you from the chair-lift. Keep going without stopping until the bottom of the slope if you get that far!

When I'm acting the voice at the back I often add the comment "you're looking really smooth now, you've really got it together" and then they go to pieces as they recognise the message and try and earn more praise!

A tip for the one in front. Choose a focus, apply all your thought in that one direction: perhaps choose one of the drills we've looked at in this book. When you are totally absorbed in this way you'll never notice the comments. There's a lesson there somewhere!

SUMMING UP THE FIFTH DAY'S SKIING

I hope you have enjoyed today's games. If you've tried them all you will have had a long and exhausting day! When you don't feel happy with your skiing and are not feeling 'on 'em', pull out some of these exercises from the kit-bag and you will quickly discover the old magic.

Have you tried demonstrating any of them to a friend? That's the best way to get value. When it's your idea to 'play games' you'll notice your commitment will be 10 out of 10 and that's where the real benefit is!

Sixth Day

The final day of the programme! Today we are going to build on what we've learned and discovered over the last five days. We shall look at how we feel about skiing and about ourselves, and how these feelings can and do affect our performance.

After that, we'll go off-piste and start to explore the opportunities for fun that the whole mountain offers. Skiing is much more than a groomed piste!

Whenever you do anything on skis notice, if you can, your attitude to what you are about to perform. This attitude can interfere with our ability to perform as we know how.

Here are a couple of examples, so you will see what I mean:

1 A novice skier is standing nervously on a slope steeper than he is used to. He is 'hugging the hill', his bottom facing the valley and his lower shoulder turned uphill. Not very comfortable! His anxiety dictates his body position, which is not allowed to find its natural point of balance on its own.

If you asked this novice to step out of his bindings and to stand still on the slope you would notice an amazing difference. He has abandoned two long platforms for two short ones! Feeling confident that his boots will support him he edges them into the slope and adopts a natural, balanced position. If he could have trusted his skis in this way his body would have discovered this same natural position.

You see, the potential was there all the time, his attitude was just not allowing it to be fulfilled.

2 You are skiing smoothly down a slope when you notice a patch of ice ahead of you. In a flash you remember a bad fall you once had on ice – your attitude towards it is one of fear – you tense up, reach the ice, try to manoeuvre awkwardly away from it, and. . . crash!

Another skier seeing the ice looks instead for the snow beyond it where he knows his skis will grip. He lets himself go over the ice and leaves his manoeuvres safely

till later. It wasn't the ice that caused the crash, but the first skier's attitude to it.

How do you see yourself as a skier?

How you think of yourself as a skier will have a lot to do with your attitude to your skiing. If your image of yourself is of a hot-shot powder hound your attitude on an easy

piste is not likely to be one of fear! If you see yourself as a timid, cautious skier who feels safe only on the slopes you know, what's your attitude going to be towards skiing off-piste?

Our attitude towards our skiing dictates the degree that we doubt whether we can successfully ski the next turn. When there is no doubt, our bodies are relaxed. When we feel doubt, we 'try harder'. The trying produces the tension and this tension blocks the smoothness of the turn. Do you see the connection between:

1 How we see ourselves as skiers
2 Our attitude to our skiing
3 Our trust in our skill
4 Our stiff awkward movements/our poised, balanced technique?

This leads us back to (1) How we see ourselves as skiers!

We can break into this cycle at step (1) by pretending to be a completely different type of skier.

LET'S ACT A DIFFERENT ROLE

What role do you act out as you ski? Are you the safe and cautious type or bold and fearless?

Let's look at a few of the roles we see being played out every day on the slopes. Then we'll act each one in turn, perhaps recognising the one most like ourselves and then selecting the one diametrically opposite, to concentrate on.

Here's a chance to 'ham' it up a bit – imagine you're auditioning for a new movie! Here are some of the parts available.

1 The terrier

He doesn't want to miss any of the action. Whether it's a mogul over here or some soft snow over there, he's determined to get it all in, during one run. He always takes six turns where two would have done. He treats every run as if it was his last and spares no energy in his pursuit of 'the action'. He's only happy when he's exhausted. And he is, often!

2 The show-off

The terrier doesn't mind what people think of him, he doesn't even know they are looking. For the show-off an audience is indispensable to his act. Clothes,

equipment, sunglasses and lip-cream are his props and the slope is his stage. He looks good in lift queues and stands posing on the slopes, one ski resting on the top of the other boot. His movements are big, expansive, eye-catching. His eyes dart in all directions looking to see who's looking. A ski lift here, a restaurant there, and then as a bonus, a few turns underneath the chair. That's the show-off!

3 The meditating monk

This one knows no distractions. He skis as though in a trance, his mind in another world. He looks as if he's oblivious to the snow, the bumps and other skiers whilst calmly gliding down a pre-ordained route to his morning prayers, or perhaps repeating a mantra. There is no emotion, no hurry, no thrill. He's a calm one, our monk!

4 The mouse

Always ready to follow but never to lead. Apologises for his skiing, excusing himself for it being his first day out in two years. He admires the way you ski and if you slow down he'll be right behind you trying to pick up a tip. He doesn't like to attract attention but he'll modestly do enough to keep up. In contrast to the expansive movements of the 'show-off', the mouse is hurried, anxious with a continual frown and short jerky movements punctuated by frequent rests to check out where he is. The mouse will often have trouble with his bindings, sometimes blaming them for other problems.

6 The 'no fall' king

He has a proud record to maintain. He hasn't fallen in four seasons. He goes anywhere, off-piste, on piste down the steepest moguls, and never falls. He's as solid as a rock, skis like a tank legs wide apart and never, ever, takes a risk. Boring but reliable, the 'no-fall' king.

5 The competitor

Always wants to win, and every run is a competition. Off-piste he'll wait for you to finish your run so you can look back and watch him make 'eights' of your linked turns. On piste he'll start after you but somehow always arrive first after a near collision whilst overtaking. A companion isn't just a skier, he's somebody to ski better than! If he's not as good as you his efforts to compete will demoralise him and he won't enjoy his skiing. If he is better than you, there's no challenge, he'll soon be bored. Unless you are a competitor too, he's only good company in small doses.

7 Daredevil Dan

Never so happy as when he's on the edge of control. Always looking for the steeper challenge, the more difficult snow, the faster track. Fast schusses off-piste in 'crud' are one of his specialities but he's looking for a thrill anywhere. Nothing frightens Daredevil Dan!

Do you recognise yourself in any of these roles? See if you can act them all with your companions and guess each other's roles.

Our own role has become a habit to us. We're not likely to give it up easily. Adopting another role can give us an insight into other feelings, other moods, other techniques we might never have discovered in any other way.

You might not like to become any of these types but each one provides a lesson we can enjoy and learn from.

A CHANGE OF MOOD – A CHANGE OF HABIT

Do you find yourself skiing in the same way, run after run, constantly refining one chosen technique, ad nauseum? We need something to break out of these limits we set upon our learning and free ourselves of the habits that we so carefully make our own. You may surprise yourself. You will certainly discover a lot more learning beyond the barriers that you have put up around what you think is the 'right way'.

One way to get out of the old routine is a complete change of mood! Let me give·you an example of what happened with a group of skiers I was with recently. The group was feeling a little flat after two days of hard skiing. One person in particular was clearly becoming increasingly frustrated with his own skiing. Sensing the mood, I suggested that we do some 'method' acting.

1 "How would you ski if you were feeling extremely angry and frustrated?" I asked. They responded by gripping their ski poles tighter and stabbing them into the snow. Faces contorted with 'rage', movements were sudden and jerky, breathing became more strained. You could really see how angry they were!

2 I suggested a change of mood: "How would you ski if you were really nervous of the slope?" They were getting into the game well now, with arms and knees quaking in mock terror, legs stiffening and occasional crashes! Each was going to prove they could be more nervous than the rest.

3 "Now, imagine you are really bored, the slope is too easy for you, you can't wait to leave it to look for something challenging". The body postures visibly relaxed and became floppier, breathing became heavier and deeper, and arms swung around loosely. A completely different body position from the earlier moods!

4 "Now you are really sad, you've just heard some extremely distressing news". The 'hams' reached for their handkerchiefs and sobbed down the slope. Shoulders dropped noticeably as the group slouched into their mournful poses. They couldn't help but notice the difference: they were absorbing the bumps as if their legs were made of rubber. They were relaxed and calm. In fact they discovered 'dynamic balance' (see Day 5)! We had to ski another 'sad' run as everyone enjoyed it so much, until we came to the last 'act'.

5 "Ski 'happy'! You've just won £1 million, your financial worries are solved, and you're skiing down to collect the cheque at the bottom of the slope"! With shrieks and whoops the group took off. Nothing mattered any longer as they leapt from mogul to mogul, flung their arms high about them and just abandoned themselves to having fun!

This series of runs took about an hour. In that time the mood of the group had changed from flatness to exhilaration. They'd enjoyed expressing a range of emotions and were amazed at its effect on their skiing.

Learning and fun can come from the most unexpected quarters. We squeeze our limitations on learning and enjoyment into tight restraints to match our moods, our image, our public face. When we abandon our usual act, beware! The real skier inside you might actually get out!

The problem with expectations

We all have expectations about anything we are about to do – especially when it is a ski holiday! We expect to have fun, we expect to meet exciting people, we expect our skiing to improve and we expect good snow and good weather. We expect the hotel to be comfortable, the food good and the whole holiday to be value for money! Do you notice the reliance you are placing on factors beyond your control in order for you to have a successful holiday? With so much opportunity to be 'let down', it's a miracle anybody has any fun at all.

When it comes to a ski lesson expectations are really high! We expect the class to be small, to have individual attention, we expect to be amused and interested, we expect to be shown some exciting runs, we expect to improve. Notice who you are giving the burden of all that expectation to – the poor instructor!

Ski 'happy'!

Expectations are about passing the buck. Other people or outside factors have got to perform as we want or we'll be disappointed. What often happens? We're often disappointed!

From expectation to intention!

An expectation gives us a clue as to what we really want. Recognise the expectation and turn it into an *intention*. Suddenly, instead of relying on agencies outside yourself, you become a powerful creative force that can bring you everything you want from your skiing.

- Instead of expecting to improve your skiing, how about *intending* to improve?
- Instead of expecting an enjoyable holiday, how about *creating* it that way?
- Instead of expecting to become a fluid, balanced skier as a result of reading this book, how about *making* yourself one?

THE POWER OF YOUR IMAGINATION

What can you remember about the last time you skied. Where was it? What were you wearing? What was the weather like? Who were you with?

If that conjures up mental images for you, you are using a skill we often use – visualisation, or thinking in pictures. It can be a very powerful learning tool.

Many World Cup ski racers, having closely inspected the course, stand quietly near the top with their eyes closed. On TV it might look as if they are saying their prayers. Some may well be, but most are actually doing something very different. They are 'seeing' themselves skiing down the course. They 'see' every gate which they've memorised, they 'feel' and 'see' the line they are choosing and they 'look' ahead to the next formation of gates.

If on their internal 'film screen' they picture a fall or a

disjointed action, they will stop the film, re-run it, and ski the course again until they can complete it to their satisfaction. They will even time this process and compare their visualised time with their projected time. If it's a few seconds slower they will run it through again until it is closer.

This 'mental' rehearsal is very valuable. Many of the signals that the brain has to interpret during visualisation are the same as it will receive during the real thing. Repeatedly going over an activity in your mind helps strengthen the mind's ability to handle the same activity when it is 'for real'.

Most top-flight athletes use some visualisation in training and as preparation to performance. Like any skill it has to be practised. The more accustomed you are to doing it, the easier it will be and the benefits to your skiing will be greater.

You haven't done anything in your life yet, on purpose, which you haven't in some way visualised doing beforehand. Let's now use this ability to increase our performance, not just to repeat old patterns but to break out of self-imposed limitations and reverse bad habits.

How can we master the skill of visualisation?

For skiers there are two ways that visualisation can be a very valuable learning tool: PRE-VISION (before you perform the action) and REPLAY (which gives you the feedback after the action is over).

YOUR IMAGINARY SLALOM

1 Stand at the top of a slope and set yourself an imaginary slalom course. Make it as easy or as difficult as you like.
2 Once you have decided where to put the poles, close your eyes, exhale deeply, and see yourself skiing your 'course', just the way you would like to ski it. Feel the wind rushing past your face, see the poles brush past you on either side, see the line you make with your skis as you weave a path through the poles.
3 Are you seeing and feeling the action from within you, or are you seeing yourself from outside? There is value in both, but when you rehearse the action from within the 'feeling' senses come into operation too.
4 When you can see yourself skiing the whole slope and you are happy with it, open your eyes and immediately ski the slope for real.

REPLAYING THE RUN

1 After finishing a run, close your eyes and replay the run in your mind.
2 When you can see the whole picture, focus in on detail. Where were your hands? Where was your weight? Could you feel your shoulders? What was your head doing?
3 Pick up on any aspect of your skiing which wasn't clear, you couldn't remember, or you weren't happy with.
4 Replay the run again, this time allowing the feature in (3) to behave as you would like it to. If your head was nodding you might like to visualise it being still; if your arms were stiff, visualise them relaxed.
5 You have now built up the pre-vision for the next run – continue the cycle!

Feel at ease using your pre-vision and replay techniques. They are one of your greatest individual learning tools. Get used to running quickly through your 'films' before and after every run; it will accelerate your improvement.

SKIING THE OFF-PISTE

For many skiers the only sport is skiing off-piste. For those who haven't ventured off-piste it's impossible to describe the excitement and thrill of skiing over, or in, new untracked snow. Seeing the amazing efforts and expense that many take to enjoy these thrills – from chartering helicopters to rising at 6 a.m. and walking uphill for five hours – there must be something in it! There is, and I'd like you to join me in discovering it.

A FEW MYTHS UNMASKED

There are more misconceptions and myths about off-piste skiing than any other aspect of the sport. Let's look at a few of them:

1 *It's only for experts!* This is how many skiers, brought up only on the piste, view the off-piste. Traditional ski instruction tends to keep on the piste except for the highest standard groups. Skiers see learning as a progression of standards with off-piste skiing at the top! The off-piste is for everybody, and on our courses even beginners within a couple of days will have experienced their skis running through untracked snow. For them off-piste is just a different sort of snow.

2 *It's very difficult.* The snow is not difficult, it's just being snow! There seem to be two main reasons why so many skiers perceive it as difficult:

- They ski in an unbalanced way, which they can get away with on the piste but quickly find doesn't work off-piste.
- They consider 'off-piste' a totally new sport requiring totally different techniques.

Of course the snow and conditions off-piste are different. The depth of snow varies, its consistency varies, the underlying contours vary, the resistance felt by the skis varies. Off-piste is about variety! Our skis and our bodies, when trusted to produce the balance and manoeuvrability we want, can adapt to all the various conditions. That is what makes skiing such fun.

The **truth** is that off-piste skiing is different. The **myth** is it requires a new set of rules to be able to do it!

3 *It requires more energy and strength.* Deeper snow does provide greater resistance to your skis. This resistance helps the ski form the arc along which we turn, as we discussed on Day 2. The pressure against this

resistance which moulds the ski into the arc comes not from us, but from our speed.

To allow the skis to work effectively you will need to 'let go' and ski a faster line than you would choose if you were on the piste.

4 *You must lean back.* Our skis are designed to ride up out of the snow if you let them. Many photographs of good powder skiers make it appear they are leaning back. This is the problem of analysing a moving action from a frozen moment in time. It ignores the skier's reaction to the forces on him which make it appear he is leaning back, though in fact he is balanced over his skis. Others

copy him by make a rule of leaning back. They lift the front edge of the ski off the snow altogether; this reduces steering and control and they end up going faster and faster. Those who have developed leaning back into an art form rely on the thickness of the snow to be their control factor. Would you like to aquaplane in your car along a wet motorway relying on your hand-brake for control?

A CAUTIONARY NOTE

Before we go off-piste, one or two words of caution and advice.

1 The piste patrols in ski resorts do not check off-piste runs. Never ski alone and preferably in a group of at least three. In the case of an accident one skier can go and raise help and the other can stay to support the injured.
2 Stay within sight of a piste unless you are with a local guide or someone who knows the area well.
3 Avalanches can trap all skiers on a mountain. Those on piste are not free from risk but for those off-piste it is greater. If you have the slightest doubt about the stability of the snow, *don't go.* Always ask local experts for their advice. Judging avalanche conditions, though a science, is not a precise one and the experienced skier always errs on the side of caution.
4 If you fall and lose a ski in the deep snow it can take ages to find it again. If that happens to you, nine times out of ten you'll find it buried at the very beginning of your fall, though you may have to climb back a long way to get to it! If you wear ski straps you won't lose your ski but you risk cutting your head open with a flying ski. I prefer to use a length of red cord tied to my ski which trails behind it up to the surface (I hope) in a fall.

OFF-PISTE EXERCISES

Off-piste you have the ultimate test of whether you really are trusting your body to balance you and your skis to turn you. Anything less than 100 per cent for either and you'll know about it!

Many of the exercises and drills we've explored are equally applicable off-piste. In powder, because we are not skiing on a solid base, we need to develop increased sensory awareness through our feet. Compare bouncing up and down on a hard surface with bouncing on a trampoline. It is a different sensation and we will only be able to handle it by increasing our awareness of the difference.

It's OK to fall!

By the way, it's OK to fall! Anybody who is going to improve their off-piste skiing is going to fall a lot. Don't equate your skill in the powder with your frequency of falling. Four linked turns where you've let go and 'gone for it' can, in spite of a crash before the fifth, provide more satisfaction than a complete day spent struggling to stay upright!

Here are some of the exercises and games I find especially helpful in the off-piste.

THE POGO STICK

Whilst traversing a slope, hop up and down as if you were on a pogo stick. Feel the snow beneath you and the difference in textures and resistance. Begin to recognise the varieties of snow and to read them with your feet. If you feel the skis turning, let them. If they are not don't make them, just see if you can pick up the rhythm of 'bouncing in the powder'.

THE COMMITMENT SIDE-STEP

As we did on page 59, do the commitment side-step with the uphill ski and see what happens. Do you see why it should be any different off the piste than on it?

How much do you trust the ski to take you round?

DON'T FORGET TO BREATHE!

1 Check your breathing by exhaling and noticing it.
2 Try counting, shouting "NOW" or blowing the candles on a birthday cake each time you begin a turn.
3 When you see a good skier off-piste, listen to *his* breathing pattern as he goes past!

TAKE A LOOK AT YOURSELF

1 Before you ski the slope ahead of you, take a moment or two, close your eyes, and visualise yourself skiing the slope as you'd like to.
2 Open your eyes and ski it.

It's OK to fall...

...and fall...

...and fall

HOLD ON TO YOUR HULA-HOOP

When we discover a slope which no one else has skied, we pause at the top excited at the prospect of making the first tracks down it. Then the interference starts. "Am I going to fall?" "How many turns will I do?" "What will I look like?" "Should I go first or let my companion have the first crack?" "I mustn't mess this up!"

We all have some thoughts like these going through our heads at the beginning. When we've got going, the magic of the moment takes over; but to get along, just for those first few turns whilst you are finding the rhythm – **hang on to your hula-hoop** (page 76).

FINISHED WITH YOUR TURN?

At what point is the turn finished and the next one not yet started? On the piste it is just possible to be skiing one turn while you're still thinking about the last one. This practice is not recommended off-piste. You lose the very sensory awareness you want if your attention is always three seconds behind. You know this has happened when you complete three linked turns and on the fourth you disappear at a tangent at high speed!

Recognise where your turn has finished and stand up as if to 'take a bow'. The next turn is in the future and the last turn is in the past. You are now in the present. As you stand up say "NOW" to demonstrate that at that point you've let go of the past and are prepared for the next turn. This is a vital aspect of your off-piste skill. Check it out on the piste, recognise the point at which your turn is complete (physically and mentally), and then look for it off the piste too.

THE COUNTDOWN

There's a game and a challenge in every run. Counting your turns helps you to:
1 See where you are with your skiing (a 'five rating' or an 'eight rating').
2 Set a target, say four turns more than you rate yourself.
3 Exhale on the turns.
4 Show off, if you are into that too!

All off-piste skiing provides a great challenge to our balancing skills, our awareness of the snow, and our reactions to it. Every run presents a new challenge. When you have discovered the freedom of the off-piste you will have discovered the freedom of the mountain.

How would it feel if you were 25 kg lighter?
Skiing off-piste seems to take an awful lot of effort at first until you discover the rhythm of it. After doing any of these exercises, ask yourself "How would I have skied that if I were 25 kg lighter?" and ski it again as if you were!

Do you feel a difference? It sounds glib to suggest an exercise like this when you are reading it from a book. But go out and try it. How *would* you ski if you were 25 kg lighter?

How would you ski this slope if you put in half the effort?
Another question for your imagination to play with but with instant feedback too. Skiing is not about putting in a lot of effort. How would you ski the next run if you put in half the effort?

94

SUMMING UP THE SIXTH DAY'S SKIING

Today we discovered how powerful an effect our attitude, mood and even our character have on our skiing. Recognising this effect brings us closer to understanding and solving the mysteries of learning to ski.

Your potential as a skier develops more productively in a supportive environment, when your 'mental approach' is in harmony with what you want to achieve. Now you need no longer be at the mercy of your mental attitude – you can choose the role you want to play!

I hope you enjoyed the off-piste skiing. I would have liked to introduce it earlier in the week, but the principles of our approach are perhaps more quickly appreciated in a 'relaxed mode' at first, which for most skiers means on-piste. But I hope you will continue to explore the myriad possibilities of the off-piste and enjoy the constantly changing variety and challenges it offers.

A FOOTNOTE TO THE SIX-DAY PROGRAMME

The learning you have been achieving over the past six days is the beginning of a continuing process. The process doesn't stop because you have come to the end of the book or the end of the programme. It doesn't even stop because you have put away your skis for the summer. You can apply the principles of what you have learned during the past six days to any sport, or indeed any endeavour where you want to fulfil more of your potential and achieve greater results.

If this book has opened up a totally new way for you to look at your skiing, that's fine! If your skiing has improved, that's good too. But if you have enjoyed participating with me in the week's programme, then my chief aim in writing this book will have been realised.

I hope you continue to enjoy your skiing for a very long time.

Ski Skills Alpine Courses

The author demonstrating commitment!

Each winter you can join our team of coaches for a week or two and ski with us in one of the most beautiful resorts in the Alps – Villars, in Switzerland.

Courses are held throughout the season and we welcome every standard of skier, the exprienced and the novice.

Just as no two skiers are the same, so no two courses are the same. The team of coaches, who come from **Britain, USA, New Zealand and Australia**, bring new **ideas each season**, though the underlying approach to **learning**, which I hope you have enjoyed in this book, remains the same.

We'd be delighted to meet you and ski with you. If you are interested contact us at

Ski Skills Limited, Ranelagh House, 52 Binswood Avenue, Leamington Spa, Warwickshire CV32 5RX Tel: 0926 831251
or cut out the coupon, return it to us and we'll send you all the details.

SKI SKILLS LIMITED, 52 BINSWOOD AVENUE, LEAMINGTON SPA, WARWICKSHIRE CV32 5RX, ENGLAND
Please send me details of your Alpine Courses.

NAME (CAPS) . . . .

ADDRESS . . . .

. . . . POST CODE . . . .

TELEPHONE DAY . . . . HOME . . . .
